The Poetry Review

The Poetry Society, 22 Betterton Street, London WC2H 9BX

The Poetry Review

The Poetry Society, 22 Betterton Street, London WC2H 9BX
Tel: +44 (0)20 7420 9880 • Fax: +44 (0)20 7240 4818
Email: poetryreview@poetrysociety.org.uk
poetrysociety.org.uk/thepoetryreview

Editor: Emily Berry
Production: Michael Sims

ISBN: 978-1-911046-12-7 ISSN: 0032 2156
Cover artwork: Manshen Lo, manshenlo.com
Cover quote by Rainie Oet, see p. 11

...

SUBMISSIONS
We welcome submissions. Please follow the guidelines which can be found at poetrysociety.org.uk/thepoetryreview

ADVERTISING
To place advertisements, visit poetrysociety.org.uk/thepoetryreview or contact Oliver Fox on +44 (0)20 7420 9886, email: marketing@poetrysociety.org.uk

BOOKSHOP DISTRIBUTION
Central Books, 50 Freshwater Road, London RM8 1RX, UK. Tel: +44 (0)20 8525 8800 or visit centralbooks.com

PBS OFFER TO POETRY SOCIETY MEMBERS
The Poetry Book Society offers Poetry Society Members a special 10% discount (plus postage) on books bought from poetrybooks.co.uk. For details and to obtain the discount code, please contact Paul McGrane on +44 (0)20 7420 9881.

SUBSCRIPTIONS & SALES
UK individuals: £38 / Europe: £48
Rest of the World: £53 (overseas delivery by airmail)
Single issue: £9.50 plus postage. Order from poetrysociety.org.uk/shop or contact Paul McGrane on +44 (0)20 7420 9881. Pay by cheque (sterling and US dollar cheques only), credit card or Direct Debit.

Subscribe to the digital version of *The Poetry Review* at exacteditions.com/thepoetryreview
The Poetry Review is on sale in leading bookshops. It is also available on audio CD.

The Poetry Review is the magazine of The Poetry Society and was first published in 1912. A subscription to *The Poetry Review* is included as part of membership of The Poetry Society. Views expressed in *The Poetry Review* are not necessarily those of The Poetry Society; those of individual contributors are not necessarily those of the Editor.

Charity Commission No. 303334.

...

THEPOETRY**SOCIETY**

Supported using public funding by
ARTS COUNCIL ENGLAND

MIX
Paper from responsible sources
FSC® C010693

The Forest Stewardship Council (FSC) promotes environmentally appropriate, socially beneficial, and economically viable management of the world's forests. By buying products with an FSC label you are supporting the growth of responsible forest management worldwide. The Poetry Review *is printed with vegetable-based inks. Surplus inks, plates and printing blankets are recycled.*

CONTENTS

Poems

Lecture

Reports

Reviews

Response

EDITORIAL

In December 1947, this magazine's then editor Muriel Spark wrote in an editorial, as though responding to her detractors (of which she had many), "Let us distrust the vicious, shrill, almost hysterical denunciation of an 'obscure' poem until we are satisfied that it is indeed the poem which is nebulous and not the vision of the accuser, involuntarily withdrawn from a blinding, significant light." It's somehow comforting that people are still levelling the same complaints at poetry today. What would be so bad, though, about something being "nebulous", or its synonyms, 'hazy', 'indistinct', 'uncertain', 'cloudy', etc? So much in life is all of those things. The sky today, for example, which had got right up close to the window when I pulled the blind this morning – Charles Dickens's "Implacable November weather", "a foggy glory". Or my mind, whenever I'm called upon to sit down and write something like this.

When learning how to meditate, one is often told to imagine the mind as a clear blue sky and thoughts as clouds passing across it. You're not supposed to think of the clouds as bad, they're just part of the deal. "The mind's white / rind, not the white / rind's mind" to repurpose a quote from Will Harris's sequence in this issue, excerpts from 'The white jumper'. In a novel I read recently, Fleur Jaeggy's *Sweet Days of Discipline* (trans. Tim Parks), the narrator observes, "I still thought that to get something you had to go straight for your goal, whereas it is only distractions, uncertainty, distance that bring us closer to our targets, and then it is the target which strikes us." 'The white jumper' leaps through scenes in which a speaker appears to be in vague pursuit of the titular object (or subject) but finds himself continually sidelined by recollections and observations; similarly the speaker in another excerpted sequence, Ralf Webb's 'Treetops', is less focused on his journey than on the thoughts and memories that rush towards him like "blurry horses".

Distraction is frequently maligned, but Mary Ruefle has written in praise of its virtues in her lecture 'Madness, Rack, and Honey':

> Sometimes I think a poem is the "essence of distraction," which is certainly an oxymoron, since an essence is that which is most concentrated and distraction so wide; in a poem life distracts us from our lives, and only with the utmost of our concentration are we able to follow the exchange as it takes place. So the kind of distraction I am speaking of is one that leads to concentration, the concentrated form that is a poem.

In his lecture on "winter words", printed in this issue, Simon Armitage talks of distracting himself through the darker days of that season with A.R. Ammons's *Tape for the Turn of the Year*, a "poetic journal" notable for its architecture, each line no wider than the till roll it was written on. Reading the poem at its own pace, one dated section per day, Armitage acknowledges, "my daily appointments with *Tape for the Turn of the Year* had the intensity and sometimes claustrophobia of a waking hibernation, of deliberately joining the poet in his slow journey through the gloomy underpass". This sounds like the kind of distraction Ruefle and Jaeggy are talking about – the kind that submerges you in something dark and nebulous in order to pull you closer to the source. Or as Harris has it "our feet in / thicket dark our heads / in thickest / stars".

Quite often, I cycle home past a piece of graffiti that says "Certainty is a trap". Each time I see it, I think about this statement, written in large white letters on a brick wall, but it won't give way. The words are inside their own trap, being, themselves, so certain. "Thought needs a trap, so we should all carry sins", suggests Baek Eun-seon in her poem 'a hospital a customer a chair a table' (trans. Jae Kim) – maybe the feet have to be in the dark for the head to be in the stars. Or maybe it's all just "foggy glory".

Emily Berry

Muriel Spark edited The Poetry Review *from 1947–49. 2018 is the centenary of her birth.*

RUTH WIGGINS

Daughters

The feral dogs can smell the glitch inside the cardboard box – two salvaged female pups, not yipping much as they are carried across the un-adopted lot, their sister discarded on the sidewalk. The tourists (like us they are here, and yet they are not) can't quite get with the programme. We have three weeks on them and watch as they make for the grocery store, cardboard crib fading in their arms. Next morning we see them outside the temple. The pups have spent the night in a T-shirt, dining on peas and tuna. A food bowl improvised from the bottom of a bottle, moulding not unlike their mother's paw print. They have a sign that reads – *TO TAKE* – a little heart to encourage the monks and stallholders. But no one wants a girl pup. In the National Gallery behind Sükhbaatar there is a bust entitled *Give Me a Daughter*. Give me a daughter, one with a soft-furred belly, fat with peas and tuna. Make her golden-eyed and skittle-legged, and with a bark to raise the dead.

A handful of string

the knot, fraying
but softened with grease
Out of which, I try to teach
cat's cradle
to Nyambuu's grandson
His small face saying
like this?
Mine – *nearly, like this*
We need a second interpreter
for this work
one for the body
My mind too slow
for fingers that know
the steps on instinct
But why a cradle for a cat?
Hard to explain
Old cat caught in a boa of string
rock-a-bye kitty cat
high in the tree
But here the cat isn't really
a thing
I've seen only one
Slinking in on the wind
hard to untangle
The translator gets that look
she is bored with the conversation
It's turned to my hair again
Everywhere an archetype
that won't translate
back home

Fingers lost
        in a rope of keratin
The boy's handsome grandmother
        is the local curd queen
Her petals, hubcaps, mandalas
        sweet and blue
        with blackcurrant
As I slip my fingers, pinch
        and drop then flare back up
        she says
        without the string
        it is a mudra
She says she once had hair like mine
That it would river
        about her hips (she signs)
        could be wrangled into a braid
        this thick
But a monk had said
        it drew bad feeling
        and so she had
        let go of it
The curd wheel in her palm
        is an eye of Tara
        bodhisattva
But there is some
        mischief going on
The seven eyes, the lotus plinth
        the monumental
        shining buttocks
I look down, pinch and slip
Nuh-uh, I say, *like this*

RAINIE OET

Caverns

1.

The wind flowers in the water of the birdbath in my hands.

Where does this wind come from? Does it start and stop?
Or keep going, around the world? The same wind, over and over, forever?

Even if it dies and dies, if the birds' eggs don't hatch…

> After you died I used to have a glass bowl I kept flowers in
> inside the freezer. Everyone in the family caught on – put flowers in,
> flowers I liked and didn't, accumulating, growing, and Mom
> bought more bowls, until the freezer was filled with bowls of flowers,
> crusts of ice, petals breaking under their own weight when lifted.

2.

I wish you could have experienced Mama's hands, warm, letting go of mine
going into the freezer to take out all the bowls of flowers, flickering rain
outside, flickering   rain   sky   pink-white
pink-white like a kind of mad laughter – and emptying their contents
into the trash, the trash bag the texture of the inside of a dog's mouth,
Luna (we got her two months after it happened),
and the pink rippling trash bag plastic rubbery
like a leaf like frozen-over petals
the way light looked on the trash bag's sides (stretched taut)

> – there were the gummy worms you loved, that turned into real worms
> in my dreams, but huge – huge worms, technicolor,
> rubbery, huge, technicolor, coming into my room, mouths open

– and then Mama held my hands again
and I was struck by how blue
they felt and she said "your hands, they're so warm."

I remember the way love looked on your face.
  Oh, when we love what we love when
    it's not lost, but changed.

3.

Big ass fugly gummy worms turned real – saying "where does the wind come from"

rolling around inside me, cavernous, aching

ha   ha   ha,   death bread, gummy soul,

worms connected into worms connected into worms
    connected into worms: technicolor, terrifying.

4.

The number 4. In proximity, hands. Frozen gummy worms falling out of a bag

into water. Into a birdbath – goodbye – the bird bath in my hands. And the world

in my Gameboy – wind – forever – not forever. Broken screen, broken fingers,

broken mouth. Wide, open, to swallow the space dreams come from whole.

– And I thought that leaving my hands left hers cold,
so cold, so so so so cold, ice cold
they froze the flower petals just by touching them, then
made them break, die, no

I Miss the Slug Ooze of That Summer You Died

I put a slug on my knee and watched it crawl down my leg.

A frenzy of night itching, blood, and waking to a constellation of scabs.

And I walked in tall grass.
And I stood so still under the sun.

I got very sick for two weeks.
I lay in bed thinking I might die too.
Silences between ice-cream truck sirens
told me hours were passing.

The family in the apartment on the other side of the wall
moved. Their black labrador got into our basement
through a hole in the wall. We kept her.

Finally, I ate a tuna sandwich with ketchup, your favorite.

Austin's little sister must have peed in the bath
while it was overflowing – lemon-yellow water
dripped through the ceiling
and puddled his basement floor.

I found a hedgehog by the dumpster,
at the bottom of a mountain of huge, fallen branches,
and I poked its bared soft stomach, and it died.

Near it was a tiny square mirror I picked up
and carried everywhere after.

For a week in late August I reflected the sun onto Austin's face
until he stopped being my friend. I knew what I was doing.

On the last day of August
I sat at my window with the mirror.
I reflected the sun into windows of 45 mph cars on the throughway.
I hoped there would be an accident.
There never was.
No. The one there was – wasn't my fault.

DUO YU, *translated by Fiona Sze-Lorrain*

Writing Small Poems Makes One Anxious

Writing small poems makes one anxious, observing water stirs troubles
from nowhere
A cynical and reckless life is no easy task
Hopeless people practise killing games
Brothers share their woes under a lamp, what can your pen
do? Writing small poems
makes one anxious, observing water stirs troubles from nowhere
Just like that, nothingness
at the heart of a vegetable, righteousness in a tree trunk
A cynical and reckless life, in the night shades of this era, the sun is redundant
and impractical

Reading Historical Annals

My heart sweetens like threads of rain
on charcoal fire. Optimism is required:
use lush leaves and branches to treat minor details,
an inscribed soup ladle for a jar of honey.
Look at him: page seventy-eight, whining in tears,
eager to return to his own corpse; after a day of toil
the executioner is eating fish at home.
This explains nothing; neither does it prove irony
or sex request. Landscapes, His Excellency,
his distant royal maternal relatives and childhood –
souls across the universe: kings from all ages.
History reflects the sky: you and I
are but the wine shop's banners in a yard.
Worse: smoke and fog, just
a difference in surname; whoever governs is the same.
Tumuli into ash, fire in a flock of goats.
For a long while he sees no one: no official, warden, or salt commissioner.
Ice freezes on his forehead, yet he can't escape
from imperial examinations, mathematics, an old teacher's pointer.

Rain Born under a Leo Sign

Tonight a high north wind blows off my cumulonimbus clouds.
(Let it escort my love away.)
Wet fallen leaves scatter over the autumn earth.
(Let it nestle against my heart!)
The calmest heartbeat is the transient silence before a storm.
A knife piercing through life comes from a dove's sad tears.
Against the backdrop of an unseen end, I've decided not to live on.
(Let him die! Let him die!)
The world of love is a deep breath that bares white bones.
Clear eyes rekindle life's embers.
Epidermis in disarray: my rage dashes around in darkness.
(Let her live! Let her live!)
Thunder rolls in viscous solitude,
grave and earnest, like from some warning of fate.

LUÍS QUINTAIS, *translated by Lesley Saunders*

A Prince in All Things

There was a prince in all things.
Cherry trees blossomed in the morning.
With the most brazen white flowers
they blossomed. Out of the primordial cyclical sense
of which we know nothing, the pulsing light
that strikes at death and the fabric
of symbols, the cherry trees blossomed.
The cherry trees blossomed with white flowers,
they trembled in the wind of everlasting morning.

It was in Japan, that dwelling-place
of transparencies and qualities,
that matrix from which trooped syllables,
demotic, hoarse, warrior-like,
O worldly ones of this assembly
of sceptics, civilitas, civilitas.
They blossomed and thrummed, the cherry trees.
The flowers of the cherry trees blossomed
in the vista that's there, must be there, in the morning.
What I came to say about this ancient place
is just this: a feverish memory
of beings who make their way through a remote domain,
still just a sign, but one with a kernel at its heart.

At the root of speech there's a taint or stain
where the cherry trees blossomed
to a melody as yet unnamed
thrumming in the mind, in my mind.

A Young Woman Sits Down Opposite Me And She Is Already Language

A young woman sits down opposite me and she is already language. Then she disappoints me with the simple song of trivial days with which she looks for work, the wage-earner's obligation to a life that will wear itself out. And then she tells me again the song that the black impenetrability of the language seems to want to blot out. I free myself from doubt. My brothers are waiting for me. Someone will tell them that I've gone on a long journey. News will come of the techno-city nightmare. I'll cry out and no one will hear me. An echo will be my only chance of being heard. There will be photographs burning next to a window. Colour disappearing. Photons implicated in the boundless violence that once upset us and now sedates us. After all, when you tore open the bag, everything was already so bad, so grubby, everything was already tainted by the bag and what was hidden, palpitating, inside it. My father would read the newspapers. His eyes would hunt for some revelation in the columns in front of him. Then he'd find nothing that could calm him. He'd throw the papers down on the table in front of him. He'd get up and leave without speaking to join the streets where the empire, now dead, was rotting away. I felt sorry for the monsters in the doorway going through the ritual of there being nothing, either inside or outside.

SAM RIVIERE

from *The Epigrams of Martial*

[27]

We may have made arrangements
it was late and wasn't there wine
I once waited at an intersection
for britney or brittany for ages
it feels like the whole universe hates you
but how can you not have learned
that there are plans made when drunk
it's unseemly to remember let alone speak of

[29]

My reputation is a book
and if you want to be my stand-in
just like I am fine
you can recite my poems
while lying on the kitchen floor at night
or you could photograph these pages
in a bookshop on your lunchbreak
but if you want to take the credit
for this style yourself
ie if you want to 'own' it
I'm afraid you'll have to 'buy' them

[31]

I promise when you cut your hair
and the curls fall
to mingle with the filthy leaves
the stares of boys and girls will arrive
like knives at your white neck
newly revealed
as if routed to their source
and with each long look
they'll style your lines again
becoming angular
as again the curls fall
your last weeks as a teenager
but slower this time
slowly like your early twenties

[33]

No matter what the loss is
crying while with friends
is always a performance
it's like bribing a witness
in the absence of evidence
it only counts as crying
if you're crying alone
and preferably in silence

[35]

I write verses for my equals
not a teacher to dictate in class
these poems' wives can't be without
a penis please or would you rather
have me write down words that say no song
who dresses in petticoats these days
anyway this law was given to the poems
of Martialis who cares unless they're
somewhat prurient you could spare yourself
the severity born of a castration complex
by letting the work stand up for itself
also don't spit my own stuff back at me

[39]

There are few here who can be counted friends
few who understand loyalty or aspire to art
few who defend and admire the virtuous
few it's simple to love and for whom
you'd happily sue and especially
few as smart as they appear
to appear and yet few
without cunning
few   if any

[47]

This is to acknowledge

that poets do admin

in 2018: *received*

[49]

It was said you would find a high level
the cars and clothes as cold and hueless as each other
the premiere slopes
on half-eaten mountains
and the secluded island
with a beach you love
its grasping shoal-waters
and the watchful stillness of the inland lakes
whose opaqueness helps you to forget the other shore
its harsh metallic aspect
green like iron or ice
but from here you can nominate the games
your mind as cloudless in the shade
as the frosted water jug
and when December comes
bringing with it your birthday
and feelings of powerlessness
this climate is yours to return to
enmeshed in the global cyclone whirl
strangely untouched
a safety born from slyness maybe
and where your legacy is laddered
but on some evening in the future

in a small wooded area beyond the ring of firelight
you will call to the stranger
who waits among the trees
with a smell recalling blueberry muffins
sudden hunger proclaiming his company
a crescent of skin revealed
by the slit in your ballgown
and the party on the beach will seem distant
its noise growing querulous like that of your many clients
having a disagreement of some sort about the government
– it seems an accusation has been made
and your presence is demanded on the carpet
if it isn't a dream
you've been sleeping all morning
in a deep pale sleep
because you are insane and deserve another philosophy
because you have success
yet do not enjoy your joy
and instead you envy every stranger
their stillness and opaqueness
and you ask them to turn out their pockets
for what remains
when the business of fame
finds a final sufficiency
and the waters fall silent

AMY CRUTCHFIELD

A Clean House

Cleaning up dog vomit, I wonder
if I really am a dog lover.
A lover of anything. The vomit
an improbable brown only found in hand knits or
in the kingdom of fungi.
It's grounding.

The sleeves of my robe retentively rolled,
I ask how Shoukei Matsumoto,
or the other monks in Kyoto,
would approach this task.

The earthly dirt
that accumulates in the soul, poisons your mind,
manifests as a dirty room.
Wipe your floor and see
when you polish the floor you shine
your heart and mind.

Cleaning up vomit reminds me of marriage (mine)
and suicide. Anyone
who'll tell you what's going on
in someone else's marriage is idle, and probably lying.
It reminds me of the time in my marriage
when I had asked,
please,
no new puppy

I was your first violin, and you mine, soaring
above the corps.
But what goes up...
The solo dissolves into the mass.

It reminds me of suicide
because that has its domestic aspect too.
Easy to dismiss,
perhaps,
when you're not the one on your knees,
who still has to live in that town,
ask for the bond.

The body, toxic
spasming
ejecta.

Something reptilian
knowing only
to void.

In Jissoin, there is a special word for the floor
polished to a lustre enough to mirror the surrounding leaves –
yuka momiji (autumn leaf floor),
yuka midori (green floor).

Eight hundred years of polishing,
cotton socks,
monks on their knees.
We don't polish the floor because of dirt.

Like an old-time detective, scenting
Prunus amara in the air, announcing –
"Cyanide", I smelt the bitterness.
"Someone had to clean up."
Thought how love can turn,
not to less love, but disgust.

In fall, the maples bleed out.
The temple floor, awash with crimson.

Prunus dulcis, the sweet sister, last thing I gave him before he died.
I had jangled in, down from the city,
asked what he wanted from the shops,
with a tone that said – ask me for anything,
please
He asked for a bag of almonds.

Why not polish the floor in your home as if you were polishing a mirror
that will reflect your soul.

In winter, the wetblack boards turn white.
Mt Hiei wears a shroud. Fusuma redefine the space:
what was a wall becomes a door,
and within their painted screen,
red-crowned cranes sky-point and spread their wings.

True in the Senses

"It is shameful for any man to write in figure and colour and not be able to strip his meaning of such decoration and say plainly what he has in mind."
– *Charles Williams paraphrasing Dante,* La Vita Nuova xxv

I have always been a liar.
Some years I lied on the page as well – but
the poem won't stand plumb – the ceiling droops, the walls come down.
Truth is ballast – without these stones
the poem is a pleasure craft, heeling in wind.
And isn't the sixth sense just this –
the sense of truth? A sense the heart knows
like a nose knows milk. Or is it the hairs
on the body's dial – measuring truth
as they quiver and lift. And you know, that I know,
that the only true I mean, is true in the sense
a heart is not contained by its ribs. True in the sense
of a hammer, sweet on its nail,
the pleasure rising
into your wrist. True in the sense that woman has a smell,
and the smell is of iron.
True in the sense of the sight of the ghost white
hair on a goat's neck;
true in the sense of a bleat; and of a blade – *la lame,*
who says what she means and
means what she says.

BAEK EUN-SEON, *translated by Jae Kim*

a hospital a customer a chair a table

You sit here.

Thought needs a trap, so we all should carry sins.

While kind faces smile in warm and safe places.

Not even thinking I should talk about what I've lost.

Not reading, not listening to music, only lying down, I look at the ceiling, and lying sideways, I look at the wall.

I take care of myself the way I would a customer.

The end in the end is enlarged.

Like it's all a game.

I despise your cleverness.

A situation is needed. There is no specificity whatsoever.

A hospital a customer a chair a table a hospital a customer a chair a table, I'm thinking.

Like an idiot. Why is the idiot acting out? they'll ask.

The hospital equipment seems unrelated to health.

I dropped a knife in the water, I wrote.

I lay down on the hospital bed.

If an animal throws up, another animal eats it.

Thinking feverishly about nothing makes it seem like the universe.

A hospital a customer a chair a table.

You sit here.

Sit and feel the cold things.

The larks are probably in a tree, and in the fall peaches will be gone.

Where have I heard it. Dropa, Dropa, I keep remembering.

The elders wake up early and have sex, taking turns.

Even that which will break assembles like it will break. Strange?

Strangely such thoughts do help with the day-to-day living.

Lonely and cold, lonely and cold wind blows.

Wondering if Rilke also thought such thoughts, but then thinking
 Pessoa is popular now.

Because I'm so fearless.

All this was your choice.

A hospital a customer a chair a table and.

Aquatic plants floating in the water.

The trap may appear abysmal, but it's not really.

While two o'clock becomes four o'clock.

While thought covers thought like powdered medicine.

I'm more or less an ancient stone.

While you don't sit, nor do you stand, and burst out crying.

A hospital a customer a chair a table.

FRED MELNYCZUK

Añoranza

For ten days and nights I slowly died
on a straw bed, in a crumbling hut,
in a forsaken village of the desert foothills.
Was the days of death and burning;
great heat engulfed the region; and many
many were taken by the fires.

I laughed in bed delirious, in refusal
of food and light; I hated everything.
Such a febrile coldness entered me;
difficult to describe,
but a blizzard swept through my veins
and my heart a pneumatic drill
that shook my bones, that shook my bed.

The old abuelas forced mass on me
for the fever was not of science.
"No mas," I croaked, "no mas, I'm dry,
I'm rope, I'm roto."
"You see? Catolico si: desaparecido"
and lapsed in love. They wept for me.
"But save your tears, or drink them."
For their village was an oven
bordered by rock and made for dying;
there its people lay, with languid fans
on bleached balconies; where below
the dogs whined for the drying puddles.

. . .

Were never days so bleak in blue;
was only hate for you that saw me through.

PASCALE PETIT

Her Flowers

Just before she died, my grandmother glanced
out of her bedroom window and saw her garden

bloom one last time – with white chrysanthemums,
lavender peonies, prize dahlias,

cascades of red-hot pokers, delphinium sparks.
Did the fireworks wake her?

Muzzy from sleeping pills, my grandmother
got out of bed and started to go downstairs,

missed her step and thrust out her hand to save herself,
but the clothes drying on the banister

gave way, and down she hurtled and
broke her neck, while bouquets of lupins

exploded into the early hours.
Each November 5th I think of the passing of one

who seemed like a god to me, her sky-high flowers
when I stood in the heaven of her garden –

the mountains of her rockery, the shrubbery,
savannah of her lawn and the honeysuckles

with their anthers of fire, their buds opening
with a thunder-crack, the fuse wire of their stems.

Her Gypsy Clothes

I used to wonder why my grandmother
stared so hard into the fire
                    even after I found the cardboard box
at the back of the coal-house
                         and drew out of it

flame   chilli   emerald
sequin sparks
        embroidered mirrors
                orbiting wraparound skirts

shawls trimmed with seedpearls
silver bangles like Saturn's rings

Her embarrassment when she caught me trying them on
and explained they were her gypsy rags
                to tell fortunes at fairs

Only at her funeral did the rumour come out –
        her birth in Rajasthan to her father's maid

I think now of my great-grandmother dancing
for her master's guests   grateful
to have her baby   brought up as his wife's

I think of the coal grease   black dust
and memories that burn   slow as anthracite

        how some colours don't fade
                however deep they're buried

how even a dowry of rags
smouldering in a box
can flare in a winter grate

and how to own the country of her birth
a woman might have to wear a fire

The Umbrella Stand

What I remember is running my hands along the hide,
how wrinkled it was, how hard the polished nails,
each big as my hand. How I used to hide inside,
until one day Daddy said I'd been crouching in
the forefoot of an elephant he hunted tigers on.
How an angry tigress had leapt onto his mount
and bit into her spine. How, even after death,
the matriarch was useful. How long it took
to scoop out the flesh, rub the interior
with arsenic soap, soften the skin by soaking
in warm water, then letting it dry in the sun,
packed with sand, coir forced into each toe.
I still play hide and seek in her, and once, curled up,
fell asleep, rocked by the sway of a stately walk.
I felt every stone and flattened bush, a trunk
lowered to caress me, the branches of Indian beech
brushing my head. And high up in the sky,
my father riding on a pad of cloud – my hero,
who killed the man-eater. I was woken by his face
peering down where once there was a knee,
him saying how much he loved me, but how
I'd have to fend for myself when he goes,
to beware of his wife, my second mother.

It was then he told me the family secret – that
our hill-tribe maid was really my mam.
Sometimes I see the tigress hanging by her claws,
the explosion of her face, the black and tan lightning
that bursts from her muzzle, and the sky collapses –
all twenty tons of monsoon grey, all the rain
that's fallen in my life since Father died.
I wake in the umbrella stand. Only, there is no
rain left, just the sun drying me out, my flesh
scooped up, sand poured in my body, arsenic
rubbed inside, my skin varnished and coated with lampblack.

FRANK ORMSBY

Towards an Elegy

If I should write your elegy,
it would be when December light
darkened the windows.
Watching light fall
on the black rocks in the bay,
the disused lighthouse
where you lived,
the green headland
where no ship ever foundered,
would be a mode
of getting used to your death.
I've been assembling you from notes –
your love of the natural world,
your tastes in music,
that line from 'Dover Beach'
where a light gleams on the French coast
and is gone. I smile to think of you,
a serious man
debating how best to live.
Should you retreat
into your lighthouse
and bar the door,
or throw the door open
from time to time,
a gregarious recluse?
How could I catch the way
your small talk turned in passing
into something large.
Once, meeting me on the stairs, you remarked:
"All laughter is sycophantic."
(I didn't laugh for days after that.)
It would be a tough assignment, friend,

to produce a life impression
neither reduced nor diminished.
May the dawn not find me here,
still gazing out to sea,
the tide swarming over the mud-flats,
the page still blank
but for the first line, perhaps,
"If I should write your elegy,"
and the last:
"You gleamed and are gone."

Dawn Chorus and Painting by Joan Miró

On my birthday I walk, barefoot, downstairs
and find your card, *The Singer* by Joan Miró, propped on the mantelpiece.
Already the day promises music, already I catch
the opening imperatives of the dawn chorus,
an avant-garde concert to rouse the neighbourhood.
The blackbird takes it away, spontaneously joyful
and soon the trees are ringing with brilliant originals,
clear notes and high-pitched harmonies.
Would you want to be elsewhere, just now, as the singers
set their obsessions to impassioned song?
Looped and lassoed, I follow, as far as I can, their mazy tangles,
strings and laces of sound I lose and recover.
Now the chorus has moved on, perhaps, to the males'
fecundity and gift for mating.
Those tireless, commanding little procreators!
Then the virtuoso stuff, motifs and riffs
and effortless duets. You want to stand and applaud
or imagine a myth for the minstrels of the dawn
to make sense of their history.

This morning, again, it is possible to believe
that joy grows irresistibly at the roots of everything,
close (forgive my invention) to that fissure in Chaos,
where the birds erupted through the last freezing tunnel
of escape from Eden. Their memories were mostly of music,
but they carried also a protective panic
that still shivers when we approach and linger.
How young are these old masters who endlessly renew
their dialogue with the air? In Miró's painting
homage takes the form of the men's bird-like features
– the open beaks, the big bird's-eye shape on the vocalist's face.
The microphones are primed, the band looks drunk
on bubbly and in the mood to improvise.
The birds, so far as we can tell, may be polishing their grace notes
or sharpening the throat-needles that skewer our attention.
They might be taking time out from a champagne breakfast
or a garden party. So the day becomes more than a birthday,
as pure birdsong lifts from the trees and Miró's band
tunes up for a lively session. If I write under your name
that it is good to be alive, I hope you won't think it
a failure of vocabulary, surrounded as I am
by such artistries of colour and sound.
Whatever the day brings, it will retain
this morning's ripe underswell, its ageless echo.

Convalescence

If you slow down first, I shall slow down with you.
We shall watch the fishermen unhook their catch.
When you stop, you will stamp your boots in the snow.
Under the maple tree, we'll find every leaf a collector's item.
We shall give my walking stick a dog's name.

FAWZIA MURADALI KANE

Paring

this should be about your hands
but I can only think   about a chair   and you

            rocking

as you set the stainless steel bowl
on your lap and lifted your knife   how you cut

your loneliness   in the daytime

with phone calls and shouted greetings
to neighbours   as they pass

while your pet hen   clucked softly
below the porch   the dog would glance at her

then settle down on the steps   both adopted strays
unlikely friends   always together   but this should be

about your hands   yet an image of a white orchid
is unfurling above its clay pot   sways

so slight   in the breeze that passes through

the pomegranate tree which bore fruit
to red ripeness only   after you had left

You will observe...

after Ross Gay

that all his life he had worked
for Texaco, not in the burning field
but as a chemist in the lab, which means
perhaps he never witnessed the thrill
of a strike. Despite our neighbourhood,
he'd allow anyone into the house
to watch tv (the first in the street). It's likely
some would have stayed, expecting to be fed
as they sat on the floor and continued
to do nothing but stare at the screen.
He taught me Arabic letters as creatures
like tree frogs, that leave wet footprints
as they leap between shade and sunlight,
into leaves of *Aleph*, *Al-fathiha*, until
alone, he whispered *Ya-sin* with his last breath.

FLEUR ADCOCK

An April Bat

From the place where you are now
you've sent me a bat. Thank you.
I looked out of the pantry window
to catch a glimpse of the sunset

(rosy-pink with pollution as it was)
and there, circling and flipping low
above my flowering trees,
apple and lilac, was this bat.

Birds, we used to send each other:
a woodpecker, a jay. But this
is for the dark time.
Don't think I value it less

for being a cliché. You know
I haven't a very original mind.
You were generous enough
to send me a thing I'd understand.

Wood Mice

They'd better stop doing that, though,
if they want to go on living here –
running up the stairs in kangaroo hops
(a big leap for mouse-kind),

nibbling at everything from stationery
to paracetamol, shinning up
the striped ladder of the tradescantia
to chew on its translucent stem-joints

as if they were celery (the cheek of it)
and playing hide and seek under the bureau;
then galloping down again, a sight to see,
their little bandy legs viewed from behind –

otherwise it's into a box with them –
a humane one, of course –
and down to the woods for a new life;
but it has been known to go wrong,

alas, O alas,
which tends to make the householder
more sentimental
than might otherwise be.

So in the meantime, pending reform,
a discreet crumble of toast
or a few peanuts under the cooker
for Big-ears in the night.

JODIE HOLLANDER

Corn on the Cob

Once she got that cob
in between her teeth,
no one could stop Mother
from that wild eating.
She'd eat and eat and eat,
and then eat some more,
she'd make a mess of corn
all over the kitchen floor.
At times she'd gnaw the cob
as if it were a bone;
then we heard our Mother's
almost animal moan –
Father stood amazed
watching Mother go;
who was this woman
he'd married years ago?
But he never said a word.
Instead his bony fingers
reached into the hot water
to fish out more cobs,
which brother slathered up
with hot, dripping butter,
then piled on her plate;
sometimes brother stroked
Mother's hair as she ate,
which often made Father
slam the screen door shut,
and mutter about Mother
to the empty corn husks.
So no one ever knew
brother was punching me,
or that he fed himself

entire sticks of butter.
Mother just kept pigging out
on sweetcorn, while
the Rottweilers growled
underneath the table,
wrestling each other
and fighting for her scraps.

VANDANA KHANNA

Brief Apocalypse

The Suitors are a mixed bag of vices and dull teeth
lined up like the rotting spokes of a picket fence.

They're ready to plant a flag in the foyer and declare
me for themselves – want to tattoo my name

on their skin, stake a claim in blue-black
on the shallow field of their wrists.

My grief, exponential, outpacing any happiness
twofold. For the first ten years, the songbirds

are out of tune and everyone's tired
of my hand-wringing. Reader, my prayers

involved too much asking. And I wasn't ready
to give up on my grief, hand over my melancholy.

It clung to my lips – a tart tangle of salt air and misery
I could taste with every lie I told myself.

This is the myth you live in now: you let them win
at anything that doesn't require you as a trophy.

They eat the mutton and leave behind bones as keepsakes.
Lime bitten between their teeth, all brute and rhyme.

The best a girl can hope for, dear one, is a brief apocalypse:
a demigod that leaves his club by the door.

Who pulls at the mean seam of night, stretching
out the stars into lines of hexameter, leaving

a hole gaping as wide as a monster's mouth
swallowing the universe whole.

Interrogation

How does the girl come to be?
Talc at the back of her neck to stop the sweat
from jeweling, to stop the black-eyed shine of the evil eye.

Is the girl beholden?
She is years of *yeses* in the making, her eyes button-shut
against the world beyond her upstairs window, beyond
the hundred jeweled and slippery eyes of an empire
sewed into her veil.

What is she beholden to?
The relentless white of empire gathering as a crown's teeth
on her head, as someone else's sweat and jewels, threaded
and pearled through every tight stitch of needle.

How is the girl to be held?
A hundred tiny threads hold her
in place: by the throat, by lace and pearl and empire.

What does she want if she could?
O, how a girl longs to hold a flame to this empire, to char
its pristine white – a threat that needs no straightening,
no hands to mend it.

How is the girl to be held?
Sewn into white, sewn into the bridal bed waiting for the thread to rend.

What then?
A tear in the fabric of empire, just a pearl's gossamer eyes
at the vulnerable neck of a girl, at the vulnerable neck
of an empire. Enough to gather the shine and sweat of a girl:
a thread, a threat, a veil.

WILL HARRIS

from *The white jumper*

1

Running and jumping from one grassy
  platform to another I stop. On
the next patch of grass. Branches so
  arranged as to focus a beam of light
on it. White and gleaming against
  the green of the grass. The white
jumper. The white jumper. The white

4

We were sitting upstairs and in the whitest end-of-day light
the walls white too it felt not just like we were above
ground but that in spite of being in Covent
Garden we were on a ridge above a
forest looking down our feet in
thicket dark our heads
in thickest
stars

5

I hadn't seen Hugo in years.

At primary school, we would stay up late and play
Sonic the Hedgehog, passing the controller back and forth
when one of us died. Run, jump, jump, run, jump, run, run.

One night, his grandma screamed at us in Urdu.
She wore a plain white nighty.

We stopped laughing, or we tried laughing quietly.

By the time we had completed a level,
we could run through each jump without looking.

6

On the way home
            I ran past a Pret,
a Spaghetti House, a Five Guys, a Bella Italia.

The path lit by the lights of passing cars,
the pith of a discarded pizza.

Pret, Spaghetti House, Five Guys, Bella Italia.

Crossing the road a car honked,
its owner shouting through his closed window
            Look where you're going, cunt.

I was looking for the white jumper.

9

The Nazis admired Caspar David Friedrich for his *blood and soil* vision.

            In several paintings two friends contemplate the moon,
which seems to be exploding.

One shows the blast in its white
heat; another has the sky a darker blue; the moon dark too.

The moon is down. I have not heard the clock. A friend rests his
hand against another's shoulder to console him.

I know that
blood stands for race and *soil* for nation but *blood and soil* makes me

think of bloodied soil. Do some people imagine themselves
in the same relation to their place of birth as *a scab* to a *wound*?

10

I asked if she was scared – my mum translating.
Of what? The *coup*. No, she was brave.

In Sumatra once, having paid our respects
at the tomb of her husband, we drove into the jungle.
Everywhere was green. We stopped by a store
and the driver left us to fetch water when
men came out from behind a truck. She gripped
the overhead handle. The white blades
of their machetes gleamed. Everywhere was green.

11

Bob recounts a dream:

I see a green meadow and a white coffin.
I am afraid that my mother is in it, but I open the lid
and luckily it is not my mother but me.

12

Bed-bound,
her hair grew
out, black
strands white
at the roots.
Later they
lay her in
a white-frilled
coffin in a
marble room
and marked
the forty days
of mourning
wearing
only white.

13

Lid and lip are little words. Little
things, too. The short *i* associated with
lightness and pith.

"The pith of my system," said Coleridge,
"is to make the senses out of the mind
– not the mind of the senses."

The mind's white
  rind, not the white
    rind's mind.

14

I want to call her closed lids
buds because shut
they look like petals
tucked away which

could at any moment
bud. At her wake
she asked for pearls
to be placed inside

her nostrils
and between
her lips
and on her lids

to light her to the afterlife
and stop her eyes
from growing in this
world again.

15

In April, children chased each other round the garden.

I thought of
                the white jumper
and
                the black hood worn by hangmen

to hide the world and keep its wearer hidden,
to denote sin and keep it out.

16

Théophile Gautier dreamed of white swan-women
singing and swimming down the Rhine, each one
whiter than white down but one among them

clair de lune, pure, trailing boreal fumes,
breasts like bunched camellias – a blanched battle
of satin and Paros marble, communion host

and candle. Of what white was her whiteness
made? Pallor of alabaster. Duvet of dove.
Lactic drop and lily. Crystal ondine. Mother of God.

17

At the end of 2001, people gathered
outside the mosque. A mother pushing a pram
held a white placard in the other hand.

I watched her from my parents' room,
the sky like drinking water through a straw.

21

Friedrich Nietzsche recounts a dream:

Once the distance between us was so small
you could have crossed over to me
by footbridge.

Cross it, I said to you.
Cross over to me.
But you didn't want to.

And when I asked again, you were silent.

Now mountains and rivers have come
between us, and at the mention
of the footbridge you cry.

22

The next morning in the breakfast queue,
the man taking room numbers asked why I was in town.
I said I was giving a poetry reading. That's odd,
he replied, and moved on to a children's writer.

At Leeds, a kid was hanging by the barriers.
The station manager stared at him. What's he doing?
Being a little rascal, said Karmar. He started
to walk away before looping back, then jumped
the barrier and ran.

Run. Jump. Run. Run. Run.

KINGA FABÓ, *translated by Andrew Fentham*

Ailo and Lajla

He didn't hold me that night.
Hard as it was, he was alone.
That moment hard as it was.

As he was in me a spring.
As he was in me a flood.
As that moment in me was.

Another of his died in me.
And me with him, not of him.
Another who in me remains.

Past Name Days

I grew up in the shadow of Anna days.
Kinga left unmarked.
The Anna-fest already in swing.

I stand in a cloak. An Anna
and an Anna and an Anna.
I exist too! No sound comes.

No words in my mouth.
I'm swallowed up. Quickly forgotten.
Corrupted by the memories.

My pieces are transported
over rivers of nothing.
My traces scrubbed away

in time for my name day
fall
ing.

RALF WEBB

from *Treetops*

[episode]

Splotches of treetops through the steamed windows.
You are riding uphill in a taxi.
Do you have thick skin. Who seated you here.
Upon whose shoulders are you being carried.
Listen to what spring has brought:
static on the radio, legs of static
reaching out, scuttling into your ears.
A police officer: murder rates
in the capital, skyrocketing!
And a doctor: this winter, the elderly,
well, it was bad. Treetops are happy
bright headaches, however. Your cotton sleeve
sticks, the fat perhaps is seeping.
Scholars in gowns are slanting up the street,
getting along fine. The prime minister [static]
is pruning the municipal trees,
shedding little green scabs all over the pavement.
The cab pulls into the hospital, as all cabs do, ultimately.

You're a real live human (old pain) carrying
the conversation, or at least listening.
Good morning, images of rings inside trees
are absolutely terrifying. Good morning!
Yes, the carousel of white coats, this entire
yawning cohort, have been acknowledged,
thank you. And gurneys on silver wheels
ricocheting down corridors like pinballs.
Mixtures of syllables spilling from mouths (inc. yours)
like wet cement. And. Treetops are beautiful

global skulls. Are you feeling quite yourself?
(Sense of Self: a fork of brittle black branches
collapsible/collapsed, shatterable/shattered
clanking around like loose change
in the cavity behind the sternum, as you slide
through the reality of hospital corridors.
Interrupt me, please, I ought be interrupted)
The doctor will see you now [rapturous applause]

So, when did you first make plans? [clipboard]
Well what can I tell you, the decent die, also
the just-good-enough, &c. What else.
An unfair town. Would get dumb with weed,
whatever, and look at dreamy valley mansions:
"What parties they must have! [Classical poses]"
Our house was full of smashed crockery,
heather hung from the beams, perpetually
from the beams, dripping luck, not necessarily Good.
Sparrows nested under the roof tiling,
bees settled efficiently in the ceiling
above the bed, their geometric drone seeping
into dreams, making dreams quiver and blur,
dreams of blurry horses. Well what can I say.
You end up sinking money into a house
and then it, and its inhabitants, are sunk.
Eventually all of us will answer a phone call
and thereafter be afraid of telephones.
Timber poles standing flush against treetops,
in dark red valleys, in vines and vines,
their wires transferring ellipses which end
with extensions of sympathy. (Interrupt me?)
Hum. Life is very hard. There's no way
to articulate the terrible communal mesh.
Early this spring, a man sitting wrecked

on the fire escape asked me where the nearest
high bridge was. I told him, and the rain
fell in itchy fingers [clipboard]. For weeks
I searched the local papers for suicides.

[episode]

Bite the tape and have it wrapped around
the wound, by sundown, buddy. Carvings;
white shirts. You have seen so many things, etc.
Hello, switchboard? *Get me the engineer.*
These toy soldiers are covered in dust.
There is a weight that will not budge.
Switchboard switchboard, the tap in the basin
won't stop dripping. *I won't stop dripping.*
Debt, shifts. Winter is half the year every year,
the rest is a blend of haze and treetops.
Rota rota rota. The rain (laughter)
might look nice pummelling the fire escape.
The light, dog-rose and drunk, might look nice,
and evergreens hold your attention
for a little while, but. The omens are always bad.
Inasmuch as good ones mistrusted. Rota rota rota.
Operator: – *are third in the queue*. Stories
are useful. What happened: the unit unravelled
and its constituent parts slept in different rooms.
You stopped being able to find things funny,
ha-ha funny, anyway. Several deaths
and their associated costs; a collapsed house.
A heartbroken person leaning against
the trunk of an oak, chewing ice, tearing up
clumps of bloody grass and dirt. Wretched.

There was no more talking back, except to walls.
And you grew up, to become second in queue.
Quotes are useful, for the record: *I thought*
about my life choices, and concluded that this
was not a wise choice, but did it anyway,
persons being frequently unwise.
The pills went in the river with the till.
The charm of the other options wore off;
you went out shopping for knives.
Hesitation, then digging in – a separation,
hot butter, of yourself from yourself.
None of you, actually, thought this would be
a good idea: the vanishings in the basin.
You are yourself a new form of torture.
The carvings have left a bad pattern,
like sleepers on a track. Ha. Operator: *Hello* –
Now you are first in line, at last,
and the inky expanse of your life
with its sinews and flares, its
memories of bare lightbulbs on night porches,
memories of budgets and telephones off hooks,
memories of intolerable eruptions of love –
charges directly towards you, blurry horses.
Hello. Hi. There are some things
I would like to talk about now, please.

Dawn Nurseries & Garden Co.

At the perennial nursery: Here Good
Soil Sold. Saturday,
mid-winter, and buyers are scarce.
The few that pull up
are received passively,
like something administered.
A dog – it seems a stray –
sits on a stump, with its white eyes.

The widow who lived
in the dilapidated pebbledash bungalow
passed away two weeks ago.
The neighbours – thinking of this
as a generous grace period –
peer through the pane glass,
eyeing her antique rattan chair
and speculating about the will's executor.

A car parked beneath the overpass.
Cow shit, canisters and plastic bags.
The vehicle rocks – two fists
pop out of the sunroof and split open,
fingers desperately searching
for purchase. Nearby, scabs
of deserted machinery. A man,
all corduroy, crouched in the parsley.

CHRIS RICE

The Letters

i.m. Matthew Sweeney (1952–2018)

For seven months I've seen you
on a winter's evening in the rain
waving from a London doorstep,
anxious to be going for a drink.

Twice a month I clear the sand,
watch your airmail conversation changing:
"Love from both of us" becoming
"from us three".

In a week we'll meet again
around a glass-ringed table,
rained-on scarves and overcoats
steaming on hot pipes, talking

not of fatherhood or Egypt
but of – what else? – poetry.

In your eyes my home is nothing
but a square inch on a map.
Still, I'll keep your letters here
to read again on my return,

feet up on a plump red sofa,
fanning fruit flies from a face
whose nose has eyes and sees
in sun the perfume of the mango,

your bearded laughter once again
a flash-lit pose, a frozen wave
that twice a month I clear of sand,
waiting for more letters to arrive.

Lecture

UNSEASONAL PRODUCE

Winter words in various moods and metres

Simon Armitage

To write in winter is a contrary endeavour, an act of resistance. It involves crossing the season's picket line to access the icy workshop, creating lifelike things when so much of what is living is being taken away, rubbing the hands together for warmth when cold has entered the bones, and striking sparks into damp kindling when the planet has turned its face from the light. It's a contradiction poetry has not been able to resist.

During the previous winter, by which I mean the old-fashioned calendric winter, when the nights of lowest temperatures and the days of longest darkness used to reliably coincide, I reread *Tape for the Turn of the Year* (1965) by the American poet A.R. Ammons. I've spoken before and elsewhere about how I became drawn to mid-century American poetry, finding it a breath of fresh air compared to the clubby standoffishness of certain strains of British poetry of the same era, the fresh air being the frontier of the empty page, there to be explored and adventured along, and the breath being the proximity of the written word to the spoken language, where colloquial registers, local rhythms and quirks of dialect were celebrated front and centre rather than being tolerated as eccentric outbursts or stifled altogether. What I heard and what excited me was the voice rather than the intellect, and although Ammons wasn't by any means the most vernacular or demotic of his peers, and in some instances one of its more cerebral practitioners, I fell originally for the languid, conversational charms of his poem 'Corsons Inlet'. Having released himself from the burden of form, from what he calls "the perpendiculars, / straight lines, blocks, boxes, binds / of thought", the poet continues his free-verse wandering and wondering along the New Jersey shoreline, relieved that "Overall is beyond me", liberated from the responsibilities of summary and conclusion we associate with the bards of yore.

The titles to the poems in *Tape for the Turn of the Year*, which are really subtitles in the form of dates, imply entries in a poetic journal, beginning on 6 December 1964 and ending on 10 January 1965, a continuous daily record with the exceptions of Christmas Eve and Christmas Day (when we might assume Ammons had other claims on his time and/or other things on his mind), and 29 December. I approached the collection as if it were a kind of advent calendar, dutifully opening each poetic window on its corresponding date, and encountering entries ranging from half a page to a dozen or more pages in length, often commencing with a matter-of-fact weather report. Harold Bloom said of A.R. Ammons that his poetry "helps me to live my life" – quite a claim – and crudely speaking I suppose I wondered if it could do the same for me, either emotionally or practically, on a day by day basis. But it isn't the diarised format that gives the poem its energy and frisson, so much as its means of production, by which I mean the roll of adding-machine tape on which Ammons composed. The poet acknowledges to his readers and to himself the potentially synthetic and gimmicky nature of such an approach in the opening section, confessing:

> I'm attracted to paper,
> visualize
> kitchen napkins
> scribbled
> with little masterpieces:
>   so
> it was natural for
> me (in the House &
>   Garden store one
> night a couple weeks

ago) to contemplate
            this roll of
adding-machine tape, so
narrow, long,
unbroken, and to penetrate
            into some
            fool use for it: I
thought of the poem
then,
but not seriously: now,
two weeks
have gone by, and
            the Muse hasn't
rejected it,
seems caught up in the
            serious novelty:

A serious novelty indeed, determinedly quotidian and playfully mundane at times, introspective, philosophical and melancholic at others, the tape with its finite but unknown length representing an exploration of stamina and dedication, as well as imposing unusually slender constraints on the emerging poem. It's a limitation that forces Ammons into making spontaneous and improvised decisions in regard to line breaks and layout as he slaloms down a seamless 'page' about three inches in width, the colons he prefers to full stops emphasising the continuous forward motion of the exercise. The mention of "House & Garden" might seem throwaway but actually sets up one of the poem's ongoing dichotomies, between the domestic life of the writer – much in evidence here – and the world through the window, the outside where winter sets in, into which the restless imagination and sometimes the body must roam, and from where they must return. In that respect *Tape* is long poem of inner and outer journeys, with the *Commedia* and the *Aeneid* and *Piers Plowman* and even *The Pilgrim's Progress* as shadow narratives, but in terms of its quest for home and the meaning of home, always with Odysseus as a travelling companion. In one of the poem's few direct quotes and in staccato, one-word lines, Ammons's wife Phyllis becomes a sardonic but nevertheless telling Penelope, when she calls her husband to the table, saying:

"You
can
come
sit
down
now
if
you
want
to."

Odysseus's journey to the underworld also seems present in several passages via the occasionally elegiac or funereal tone. On 29 December – the third of the missing dates – Ammons couldn't keep his rendezvous with his "muse" because he attended a memorial service to William Carlos Williams in New York, which he describes the following day. Earlier, on 8 December, Ammons watches a violent storm on the Atlantic horizon and ruminates on the nature of fate and prophecy. The following day he reports how a plane carrying eighty people was brought down by the distant weather. Spontaneously, and as if turning to the adding-machine paper for its intended and dispassionate purpose, Ammons then presses down on the 1 key eighty times, until a cemetery of upright digits or unmarked graves has reached its tally, each figure registering an anonymous embodiment, or memorialising a lost life through an expression of cold numerical fact.

Elsewhere Ammons is an unacknowledged Theseus equipped with Ariadne's thread, using the tape to navigate his way in and out of the labyrinth of winter and through the dark tunnels of his thoughts. It's hard to do justice to the poem by simply talking about it – there's something experiential in its flow and direction, something in the silent reading of it that reproduces the process of its construction, all the self-conscious wobbles and existential balancing acts that must have taken place as Ammons negotiated the treadmill of the 'page' or performed his poetic log-rolling act with the spool disappearing beneath him. And nowhere are those feelings more present than when the poet notices a red edging to the paper indicating that time is running out, and sees the end of the roll lifting from the floor, rising to meet him. The peculiarly extruded poem has served as a handrail or safety rope through the dead of winter into spring, but the death of the poem waits at the far end.

I wouldn't want to give the impression that all I did during those short days of last winter was read, or that all I read was poetry, or that the only poet I read was A.R. Ammons, even if my daily appointments with *Tape for the Turn of the Year* had the intensity and sometimes claustrophobia of a waking hibernation, of deliberately joining the poet in his slow journey through the gloomy underpass, though when I did open other books it was mainly with the intention of complimenting or complicating and sometimes contradicting the experience with other winter poems.

. . .

If many biographical accounts are to be believed, Housman was an unlovable individual, an intellectual snob and dedicated misanthropist who emitted a virtually tangible air of disapproval and existed within an almost visible aura of unapproachability. Frogmarched along to the T.S. Eliot Prize readings or Poetry International for example, I imagine him sitting at the back of an auditorium in a pose of expressive isolation, rolling his eyes and harrumphing at the half-witted attempts of today's supposed literary heavyweights. Press-ganged into witnessing a performance poetry gig I picture him in the wings of a stage or standing in a muddy field, regurgitating his elevenses. I see him in this hall today, or rather the empty chair where he sat for a few seconds, already on a train and halfway back to Cambridge. But even when Housman was trying to be as disagreeable as possible it's difficult not to agree with some of his observations, his 1933 Leslie Stephen Lecture being one example. Better known by its title, 'The Name and Nature of Poetry', in its closing paragraphs the lecture departs from the usual customs and courtesies of academic objectivity as Housman describes his own writing practice, beginning with a pint of beer at "luncheon" followed by a two- or three-hour walk "looking at things around me and following the progress of the seasons", during which poetic thoughts would sometimes and unaccountably "bubble up". We're familiar with his description of poetry as a "morbid secretion" from earlier in the same lecture, but this is poetry as a gaseous emission, and if his remarks were judged vulgar and inappropriate at the time I can only assume that was part of Housman's general mischievousness. Likewise, and continuing with the gaseous emission analogy, if the wider tone of his oration was designed to get up the nose of those in the audience, it seems to have worked; I.A. Richards was reported as saying that it would take poetry twelve years to mend the damage that Housman had caused in an hour, an anecdote Housman was pleased to record and repeat. His headline points, however, such as they are identifiable, are persuasive and pertinent. Poetry as a subject is impossible to define, he maintains, or rather "the legitimate uses of the word [...] were themselves so many as to embarrass the discussion of its nature", though we shouldn't compound the confusion by attaching it to writing not worthy of its name. The eighteenth century couldn't write poetry, Housman tells us, breezily dismissing a hundred years' worth of the likes of Dryden and Pope, because cleverness had got in the way, a repressing intelligence and snivelling wit that meant poetry "could not describe natural objects with sensitive fidelity to nature" and "could not express human feelings with a variety and delicacy answering to their own". Three centuries later, the poetry of learned scholars is still disadvantaged by the emphasising of erudition over articulation; ironically, poetry that goes out of its way to be anti-intellectual also suffers for similar reasons, when it privileges the message over the means. "Poetry is not the thing said but the way of saying it", pronounces Housman, finally getting to his point. If that's controversial or opens up the possibility of some uncomfortable truths, it's a discomfort I recognise. A bad poem isn't just unconvincing, it actually provokes in the sensitive reader an antipathy towards the very idea being expressed, no matter how acceptable the subject matter or how laudable its standpoint. Equally, on those occasions when I've read a poem whose outlook I disagree with or even find obnoxious, a well-turned phrase or felicitous construction of language conjures a positive response somewhere in the neural pathways. So if you want me to sign a petition against the unnecessary felling of trees in the Sheffield suburbs, don't write a clumsy sonnet or some shouty protest piece about a sycamore – psychologically I'm going to turn up with a chainsaw. Instead, lure some hapless council bureaucrat into composing an excruciating ode on the dangers of falling branches and the health and safety implications of tree roots protruding through pavements in residential areas, and I'll be there on the barricades, I'll be hammocked in the boughs.

Requested to supply a definition of poetry, I think by an American publication, Housman says, "I replied that I could no more define poetry than a terrier can define a rat, but that I thought we both recognised the object by the symptoms it provokes in us." His example of this kind of instinctive and unstoppable canine/rodent identification he gives as the seventh verse of the forty-ninth Psalm of the *Book of Common Prayer*, "But no man may deliver his brother, nor make agreement unto God for him." Of which Housman wrote, "that is to me poetry so moving that I can hardly keep my voice steady in reading it." Another much-repeated example of the usually aloof scholar-poet expressing his emotions in public was recalled by a former student, who remembered Housman ending a lecture with a reading of one of Horace's odes followed by his own translation. "That [...] I regard as the most beautiful poem in ancient literature," said Housman, allegedly, apparently on the brink of tears, before he left the room. The poem was *Odes*, IV.7, 'Diffugere Nives', which in Housman's version begins,

> The snows are fled away, leaves on the shaws
>   And grasses in the mead renew their birth,
> The river to the river-bed withdraws
>   And altered is the fashion of the earth.

If the anecdote is to be believed, and if Housman was a practitioner of his preachings, then it's the wording and rhythm of the original rather than the outright meaning which he found so appealing. As someone illiterate in first-century BC Latin it's an experience I can't share or comment on, though with just a pocket dictionary and a decent internet connection I can determine that his translation is somewhat free, as poet-to-poet translations must be, and certainly has enough poetic agency and authority of its own to activate Horace's thinking. In a lesser poem, for example Wordsworth's scandalously cheerful 'Written in March', the arrival of spring stirs the spirits in the poet's breast and is a straightforward augury of health and happiness to come. "Like an army defeated / The snow hath retreated", carols the optimistic Romantic. In Horace the green shoots of spring are but memento mori. The world renews but man doesn't, and false hope is what lies beneath the blanketing whiteness. "The changing year's successive plan / Proclaims mortality to man", is how Samuel Johnson renders its moral lesson, reorganising Horace's dactylic quatrains into clanging couplets of parade-ground iambic tetrameter, quick, clean and clever but endorsing Housman's point about the eighteenth century favouring the brain over the soul. In fact the true virtuosity of the poem lies in its slide from the pastoral to the interpersonal, albeit via mainly mythological characters. In Housman's version it concludes: "And Theseus leaves Pirithöus in the chain / The love of comrades cannot take away", lines presumably haunted by Moses Jackson, the unreciprocating love of Housman's life to whom the poet was perpetually shackled and from whom he was permanently bereaved. *Odes* IV.7 opens as a flower might, waking to the spring, full of the equivalent poetic promise. But we have been deliberately misled; the snow was an anaesthetising, numbing element, and sensation, when it returns, brings with it painful truths. As painful as a returning memory after Eliot's "forgetful snow".

...

We know from the sentence-making in Thomas Hardy's prose how well he could fashion a clause or paragraph, and how smooth and clear the words could run in his shaping of narrative, or in his observations of action, or in his portrayals of a character. First and foremost the readers of his novels wanted story and plot, but having satisfied their needs and the demands of his publishers, Hardy indulged his own preferences as a writer, initially in the off-hours and by moonlight, and eventually to the exclusion of prose altogether. And the poems feel to be developed out of a different lexicon, as if in constructing verse Hardy reached for a different dictionary, on a higher shelf. Or perhaps like most poets, Hardy was simply aware how conspicuous and exposed poetic language becomes on the page.

It sounds odd to say this of a man born in 1840, but Hardy's poetic diction was always somewhat old-fashioned, and his delivery could on occasions, as Tom Paulin has noted, carry "the glib sonority of a young man trying to sound old and disillusioned". It was a poetic tone he maintained across the better part of seven decades and one that he grew to fit, so by the time of his death in 1928 his quirky grammar and peculiar vocabulary seemed not so much archaic as arcane, the idiolect of an eccentric genius with a biblical eye for lesson and parable, writing in a language of which he was the last surviving speaker and to which only he was entitled. Yeats and Frost seemed modernist by comparison.

I see Hardy the poet as a kind of cottage-industry cabinet-maker, using inherited tools and time-honoured techniques, operating alone in a lean-to workshop behind the house, someone with a devotional respect for the materials he worked with and whose products were antiques the minute they left the workbench and the varnish had dried. If all that makes Hardy sound like a servant to "the perpendiculars, / straight lines, blocks, boxes, binds / of thought" as A.R. Ammons put it, and a disciple to the set-square geometries of his architectural training, it was his knack of incorporating reclaimed timbers and found materials into his designs that separated him from other craftspeople of his time. Those eccentric inclusions come in the form of words like "chancefullness" and "undecreased" and "Powerfuller", words that warrant a ticking off from Microsoft's spellcheck function and feel as if they belong to some provincial and uncorrupted dialect of Middle Earth. Those three examples are all taken from his first volume, *Wessex Poems and Other Verses* (1898), but "Unnoting" and "deedily" and the near-unpronounceable "precienceelessness" from his posthumously published collection *Winter Words in Various Moods and Metres* (1928) prove he was still at it right to the end. And the consistency worked in both directions, in the sense that the "Various Moods and Metres" could apply to every period of Hardy's poetic output and all of his collections, the moods being anything from joy to misery (though more usually misery), and with Hardy always ready and willing to jump between autobiographical incidents and third-person recollections, between real-time observations and recalled anecdotes, and between personal confession and dramatic monologue or dialogue, though the voice is always recognisably his. As for the metres he worked in, they are as numerous as the physical shapes of the poems on the page, but it's the metrical variation within the poems as much as between them that sets Hardy apart. To express this in terms of the cabinet-making metaphor, if Hardy's symmetrical and right-angled stanzas are the solid oak drawers in a bureau or dresser, and his rhymes are the dovetails and wooden dowels and mitred corners by which the structures interlock, and his trademark indents are the decorative scrollwork and bevels, then it's the rhythmical subtlety within the poems that represent his individuality and stop him becoming the automaton apprentice to some great master or house of design producing piece after piece of indistinguishable perfection. So even though the eye perceives something of proportion and measure in a Hardy poem, the ear recognises a more nuanced construction: rarely do the poems stride along to a repeated and regular bang of the drum from beginning to end, and where rhythms do form a sort of backbeat, careful word-choice leads to restrained and understated subversions.

Hardy correctly predicted *Winter Words* as "being probably my last appearance on the literary stage", but the winter words I really want to ponder come from his previous collection *Human Shows, Far Phantasies, Songs and Trifles* (1925). The later volumes form a lesser-studied area of Hardy's output, at least in comparison with the guilt-ridden poems from *Satires of Circumstance* (1914), occasioned by the death of his first wife, Emma Gifford, or the early pieces that have the big subjects of war, religion and politics more directly in their sights. That said, the weather in Hardy is nearly always portent and symbol and often plays a political role. After centuries of land-grabbing by the aristocratic and the elite, and given continuing fashions among the gentry for transforming heaths and wetlands into croquet lawns and boating lakes, the unpredictable and ungovernable character of the skies and seasons is a rascally and rebellious presence in the work, an irrepressible voice and one which speaks with the elemental authority of the natural world, redressing the haughty chatter of the metropolis.

Human Shows isn't entirely seasonally ordered but the position of dozens of weather-related poems suggests the calendar as a rough template for the collection. So progress through autumn might be monitored by keeping a close eye – a weather eye, shall we say – on the leaves on the trees as they turn, then drop, then rot. In 'Last Week in October' a spider's web on tenterhooks acts as an early warning system, winter's alarm triggered by a falling leaf that dangles like a convict on a noose, "mumming in golden garb". Another leaf, still green and innocent, shudders at such a prospect. If the personification is heavy-handed the implications are even less subtle. Death will come to all, and the loftiest and least grounded among us will have the furthest to fall. And in drawing a parallel between expiry by natural causes and a public hanging it feels as if Hardy has anticipated Yeats's "man has created death" declaration by four or five years; as the only creature in the universe (as far as we know) to be acutely aware of our own mortality, the idea of passing away becomes a self-imposed execution, a death sentence we have handed down upon ourselves.

By 'The Later Autumn', two poems further in, all the leaves of the previous year have become corpses on the floor and this year's crop are in the process of joining them. With an appetite for the worm and the maggot, the opportunist robin eyes the scene. This is Hardy the consummate ghoul, never better than when he's mooching about in the leaf litter of human misfortune, always a willing messenger when it comes to delivering bad tidings, particularly if the message can be conveyed with a little twist of the knife, in this case by recasting the chirpy robin – the so-called 'gardener's friend' and a clichéd mascot of a clichéd winter – as a vulture. By 'Night-Time in Mid-Fall' Hardy is in full-Gothic mode. During "a storm-strid night" the falling leaves are the very least of it: this time the roots of the trees are writhing and wrenching below ground, and in a parallel image in the second verse, those roots have become a most slimy and slippery creature. Stirred from their streams, eels wriggle out of the turbulent water, squelching under the feet and slithering around the ankles of those walking along the road in the dark. And this isn't the time or place to address Hardy's much-debated attitude towards religion, but that final line, "Church timbers crack, and witches ride abroad", juxtaposing a creaking ecclesiastical structure against rampant sorcery and delivered with some relish, deserves a paragraph of response. The poet John Wain, a former professor at this lectern, said of Hardy: "He described himself as an agnostic, but he was in many ways closer to being an atheist in the high Victorian manner, combining disbelief in God with a venomous dislike of Him for not existing." To my mind, Hardy seemed to find religion not only tolerable but a necessary part of the social fabric, especially in rural or provincial communities where its customs and traditions formed part of a benign code of living. Once in a while he also allowed himself to be beguiled and seduced by the magic of religion, as at the end of his poem 'The Oxen' when he acknowledges the persuasive power of the nativity story and his willingness to be drawn along by it. But at the institutional level religion attracted his distrust and disdain. His famous poem 'In Church', in which an egotistical clergyman is overseen reenacting a performance that thrilled his congregation, has a universal message on the theme of human vanity, but it is the theatricality of Christian worship and the hypocrisy of its doctrines and dogma which are really being lampooned. Generally speaking, Hardy seems to say that if there is a deity, which there probably isn't, He's not a deliberately cruel or vengeful one, but in a frozen-hearted and unresponsive universe it's the unsuspecting and innocent – stock characters in his novels and poems – who will suffer most.

Those autumnal pieces, 'interleaved' can I say, through the first third of *Human Shows*, bring us eventually to a more intense period of cold weather, Hardy's own *Tape for the Turn of The Year* sequence, a sort of poetic mini ice age in the form of six consecutive pieces numbered 701 to 706 in James Gibson's *Complete Poems* (1979). I've discussed the poised ambiguity of the last line of one of those poems, 'Snow in the Suburbs', in a previous lecture; on this occasion I'm interested in the transformative effect of the snow. Following the increasingly bleak conditions and gloomy atmospheres of the preceding poems, the arrival of winter in its most austere garb might have heralded misery and despair on a whole new level, but elicits instead a considerate human-to-animal gesture, as if this pure and primary expression of nature has bestowed an unexpected tenderness on the urban environment and softened the heart of its residents. The original manuscript title suggests the poem is set in one of Hardy's London addresses, either a neighbourhood in Upper Tooting or St David's Villa in Hook Road, Surbiton. Either location dates the event to the late 1870s; Hardy was recently married at that time, and although the poem doesn't necessarily belong to that body of self-recriminatory work I referred to earlier, it carries the same romanticised view of the past and an idealised sense of companionship, the homely and cosy "we" in the last line a declaration of domestic harmony, the joint decision to bring the cat in from the cold proclaiming a partnership of agreed sensitivities.

If 'Snow in the Suburbs' was deliberately intended as a bright beginning to the short suite of winter poems, the 'The Frozen Greenhouse', five poems later, is its morose counterpart, an example of frost having "a curious effect on my mind" as Hardy put it in a letter to Florence Henniker, foretelling something of a "tragic nature". No illuminating and dazzling snow on this occasion, just a murderous frigidity that does for the plants in the conservatory one night when someone neglects to light the stove. Go through, Mr Hardy, Dr Freud will see you now. The poem recalls a conversation between Hardy and Emma Gifford during Hardy's visit to St Juliot church. It's a first-date poem, and the deceased plants, "iced, cold, forgot", become conveniently ironic divinations for a love that would lose its heat, for a wife now lying cold in her grave, and for a poet binging on literary remorse, his own spousal numbness of previous years now commuted to the literal numbness of Emma's body and mind. The last three lines show Hardy at his sharpest and some might say cruellest; the terse diction, the flat factual statements, the curt and clipped rhymes of "got" and "not", the simultaneous display of compassion and control, and a chilling sense of the cool detachment which is both his subject and his means of enactment.

Between the contrasting bookends of 'Snow in the Suburbs' and 'The Frozen Greenhouse' lie four more winter poems equally various in their mood and metre and in their interpretation of climatic conditions. In 'Ice on the Highway' we encounter several women arm in arm, sliding and laughing their way along the glassy road underfoot. It's a poem describing a glad and giddy scene – the women happy despite the weather. But read in combination with 'The Frozen Greenhouse' it's a poem of distant observation, Hardy witnessing joyful sisterly companionship from the position of an excluded onlooker. Of the three other poems, two concern music and the inherited significance of music in Hardy's life and writing. In Shakespeare, at night, in midsummer, the forest is a place of magic and enchantment. In Hardy's 'Winter Night in Woodland' the darkness is populated not by star-crossed lovers and roguish fairy-folk but by hunters, gamekeepers, poachers, snarers and smugglers – shadowy figures involved in shady activities, yes – but real-life people of the countryside looking to put food on the table at a time of scarcity and hardship. However, on the stroke of midnight songs are heard, chorused by named members of the Mellstock Quire from 'Under the Greenwood Tree'. In Hardy's words they sing "worn carols" brought on the air "from dim distance". It's a distance of time as much as place, the same distance that separates the troupe of passionless and penniless fiddle players in 'Music in a Snowy Street' from the "heys, crotchets, quavers" and "old notes" that Hardy associates with merry-making and dancing "when life was no trial". In both poems, music rouses in Hardy a sentimental nostalgia for the old days and the old ways. Winter is more of a backdrop or stage-set for these poems, though against its sparseness and colourlessness it feels as if the sensitivities of the poet are made keener, his nerves laid bare, his eye quick for the detail and his ear tuned to far-away noises, even to individual voices in songs being chorused by invisible members of an imaginary choir from one of his own early novels, their harmonies spanning the divide between poetry and prose.

Time is also the subject of the final poem I want to discuss, though one in which winter weather is more explicitly included and integral to its meaning. It's difficult with Hardy, or at least I have found it difficult, to accurately date the poems, and difficult to know how contemporaneous the poems are to their originating circumstances, as with 'Music in a Snowy Street', published in 1925 but presumably a version of a scene he observed on 26 April 1884 and recorded in his self-ghosted 'biography'. For that reason, I can't say for certain if 'A Light Snow-Fall after Frost', despite the "Near Surbiton" postscript, is a poem of projection or of reflection, Hardy commenting on the ageing process from a position of anticipation or experience. But with personal conviction what I can say is that it is one of Hardy's finest pieces, an exquisitely judged, enigmatically sequenced and expertly crafted conceit. If Housman struggled to recite from one of the Psalms without his voice betraying his response, I have the same problem with the first verse of 'A Light Snow-Fall after Frost', which reads:

> On the flat road a man at last appears:
>   How much his whitening hairs
> Owe to the settling snow's mute anchorage,
> And how much to a life's rough pilgrimage,
>   One cannot certify.

I won't even begin to unpack the orchestrated emotional intelligence of the diction, the syntax, the grammar, the symbolism, the cadencing, the ordering of ideas, the physicalisation on the page, the rhymes and the puns of those five magnificently composed lines – that would be an entire lecture. But to consider the poem as a whole, here we find Hardy moved and enlightened by a change in the weather; the frost, which we might read as a frosty outlook, is replaced by a soft and silent transfiguring snow, prompting an introspective response from the poet. If the first traveller on the road of life has the appearance of an older man, the fiery red beard and tree-green coat lend the second traveller a youthful vigour and vitality, though the coat is faded and the word "dye" carries an echo of its morbid homophone. The imperceptible transition from youth to old age is Hardy's theme, and the impossible task of identifying when such a change takes place. Deftly, then, instead of trying to locate that shift in his two representative travellers or letting them bear the weight of his metaphor, Hardy turns instead to the road itself, and ends with a verse equal in craft and design to the poem's opening.

> The snow-feathers so gently swoop that though
>   But half an hour ago
> The road was brown, and now is starkly white,
> A watcher would have failed defining quite
>   When it transformed it so.

There were heavy snowfalls across Britain in late December 1927 but by New Year a thaw had set in. Diffugere nives. *Winter Words in Various Moods and Metres* was being prepared for publication, and in the 'Introductory Note' Hardy had written, "So far as I am aware, I happen to be the only English poet who has brought out a new volume of his verse on his ... birthday" – the number left blank, the ellipsis a ghostly omission. Hardy died on 11 January. A.R Ammons's *Tape for the Turn of the Year* ends the previous day, winter outlived and outwitted once more, a new almanac begun, light and life on the horizon, "blessed hope" sounded by the darkling thrush, the poet turning outwards to the galaxies and away from "the warm knot / in the dark". Ammons's poem has been an act of survival and escapology, a 'performance piece' in fact, but one performed on and at and for and with the roll of paper, one the page will reenact for us as readers. In fact by the closing stages of *Tape for the Turn of the Year* it isn't clear whether poet is conversing with page, or page with poet, and whether poet or page or reader or winter has provided the contemplative emptiness in which to think and the pristine emptiness on which to write.

> I've given you the
> interstices: the
> space between
> electrons:
> I've given you
> the dull days
> when turning & turning
> revealed nothing:
> I've given you the
> sky,
> uninterrupted by moon,
> bird, or cloud:
> I've given
> you long
> uninteresting walks
> so you could experience
> vacancy:

The poem, or the paper, ends:

Thank you
for coming: thank
you for coming along:

the sun's bright:
the wind rocks the
naked trees:
so long:

This is an edited version of a lecture given by Oxford Professor of Poetry Simon Armitage at Examanition Schools, Oxford University, on 19 May 2018.

Report

REFLECTIONS OF A POET IN SCHOOL

Dai George

Poets don't always make the best teachers. By nature we're prone to introspection, cussedness, strange flights of fancy, none of which are promising attributes to admit to in the highly pressured team environment of the modern school. We're bad at behaviour management and we're not really sure of the long-term economic benefits of what we do. The problem is that the poet in school will often second-guess themselves, being doomed to straddle the dividing line between cool, interloping older sibling and qualified figure of authority. I'm not sure I've ever really learned to walk that line since I started working this beat, about five years ago – not with confidence. I value the job, value the mission, and hope I've learned to be quite good at it, but the impostor syndrome never really goes away. These are strange, fragile liaisons, infinitely hopeful though all too brief, and the fragility can feel most pronounced just at the point when the hope feels warranted: when you're on the brink of capturing that spark of creativity and self-assertion that you promised in your educational philosophy. A student shyly turns in a poem, with barely ten minutes left of the workshop. As you read it, that poem delights, surprises and moves you, rather more profoundly than you'd bargained for, yet before you can bottle this bolt of lightning the bell goes and the rest of the class are packing up, scrunching up these precious, potentially life-changing artefacts in the bottom of their bags. So you return the poem with a smile, a nod, and a platitude about how you hope they'll keep it up, knowing full well that in this very moment a sacred trust has been broached and, almost simultaneously, neglected.

Kate Clanchy is a builder, and keeper, of trust. Her new anthology, *England: Poems from a School*, presents a terrific, poignant record of the trust she has inspired in dozens of students at Oxford Spires Academy during her eight years working there as writer in residence. Those students, and the work they've created, are the product of the "magical", diverse demography of the academy, which Clanchy describes as "the chosen school of Oxford's many migrants". One takes Clanchy's point that the students' poetry is "too fresh, too moving and too compelling" for any reader – or critic – to dwell on the anthology's back story, but it would be equally irresponsible to ignore the crucial circumstances that have enabled this special flowering of talent. Supported by the educational charity First Story, Clanchy has been granted the time and latitude to establish a culture of poetic excellence at Oxford Spires, among students who countless others would write off as too quiet, too withdrawn, too disruptive, or too traumatised (many of her students come from countries wracked by war) to achieve anything more than proficiency in their adoptive language. In carrying through such a project, Clanchy has neutralised all the frenetic uncertainties that so often attend the role of the poet in school. Everywhere in this anthology – in her generous introduction and the funny, granular contributor biographies; in the evidence of her praxis we glean from the poems themselves – she upholds the values of listening, space and slow, careful attention. This book throws down a gauntlet to all educators and policy-makers who believe in the educational mission of poetry. It provides living proof that the outcomes we routinely trumpet will only be truly achieved if children are given the chance to invest in poetry seriously and consistently, over the long term.

The poems themselves – already, in many cases, stars on social media – have so far been praised in terms that risk skirting over the reality of their achievement. Philip Pullman's blurb pronouncement that they are "great by any standard" is true but somehow imprecise. Great they may be, but very often they succeed by a particular, as opposed to a generic or universal, standard. Quite simply, these poems are less inhibited, less anxious about sentiment and influence, than the average postmodern lyric. That sounds like a statement of the obvious – these are children, after all – but it can get lost in the (understandable) rush to praise these poems and welcome them into a broader community of practice. Ismail Akthar's 'I Don't Remember' proceeds by accumulating painstaking, concrete detail, organised around the paradox of what we might call the via negativa of exile, wherein acute memories of the homeland are asserted ironically, by means of deflection or refusal:

> I don't remember the place
> where the only colour I saw was green.
>
> [...]
>
> I have forgotten the taste
> of the just ripe mangoes
> which I would climb the trees to pick,
> and of fresh fish too big to fit
> in the kitchen; and of the chickens
> slaughtered in front of me, and
> of the birds, sling-shotted from the sky

I know from experience how difficult it is to get a twelve-year-old child to write with such unwavering fidelity to concrete imagery. One assumes that the poem must have been achieved using an exercise that expressly forbade abstractions, and it would certainly be none the worse for that being so. But how, then, should we explain the effect of the poem's final stanza, where all of that held and trembling discipline collapses in on itself, as the speaker submits to the familiar tell-don't-show instincts which, up until that point, the form has held at bay?

> No, I don't remember the day my life
> was taken away.
> I don't remember the fearless boy I used to be.
> I don't remember my country ...
> Bangladesh.

The ellipsis followed by the reveal is a favourite technique of young writers, and it is used here with all of its usual, childlike aplomb (and bathos). We don't want to denigrate this work by enjoying it as an endearing, risk-free category of outsider art, though to avoid such a response, I think we have to stay alive to the very difference in this writing, and thereby to the question of how it can teach us things about the common, adult practice of contemporary poetry. How might our own work have grown attenuated and diffident, too wary of the necessary emotive gesture? How can these strictures be negotiated by the simple act of publishing and honouring work that evades them?

Sometimes the poems alternate between moments of unruly, potentially gauche candour and consummate technique. Witness two couplets from 'A Glass of Tea' by Shukria Rezaei (18):

> Last year, I watched the dazzling sun dance gracefully. This year,
> the faint sun moves futurelessly.
>
> Migration drove me down this bumpy road,
> where I fell and smelt the soil, where I arose and sensed the cloud.

The first courts juvenile excess, in its alliterations and parallel adverbs (though what an adverb Rezaei has coined in "futurelessly"!); the second clinches a mature, synthesised, ambivalent emotion with a half rhyme that would make John Burnside proud. The key to properly appreciating this juxtaposition is, I think, to avoid the temptation of reading some sort of implied teleology between the first and second couplet (now she is writing like this, but soon she will be able to write like that). One should hold the two modes in complementary equilibrium, rehabilitating the double-adverb and placing it on an equal footing with the half rhyme. (And what's so great and grown-up about a half rhyme, anyway?)

A similar, uncanny permeability between innocence and experience obtains in 'Sorrow Poem' by Azfa Awad (16), which contemplates various reasons for – and figures of – crying:

> I'm cleaning up my brother's sick:
> yellow slime
> with orange bits:
> all over my flower-print
> duvet cover.

> Now my delicate brown
> hand is gloved with yolk.

That could be a Crispin Best or Matthew Dickman poem (not that Awad stands or falls by that comparison – and nor, for that matter, do Best or Dickman). There's a grisly, jingling assonance in the first three lines ("sick" and "bits", drawn together by the decomposed ballad metre), and the metaphor of the speaker's "delicate brown / hand [...] gloved with yolk" is beautiful, disturbing, and thrillingly undecided between tenor and vehicle (what, or how literal, exactly, is this yolk?). The poem nevertheless advances to a conclusion where the physical act of crying is almost too literally conjoined with its abstract, symbolic resonance:

> With stinging eyes,
> I wipe the pains
> from the ground,
> rinse them into the past

Yet in the last two lines the speaker plucks the poem from the jaws of bombast, finding a fresh and wholly unexpected solution in the very imagery and logic of crying, as she prays that her eyes will "blink me / into a brighter future". This turns into a common experience while reading *England*. The poems frequently draw impetus from cliché only to find a way of elevating or turning that cliché inside out in their apotheosis. In 'Where Are My Unnumbered Days?', Mohamed Assaf (12) ruminates on the familiar complaint of the oppressed that "I am just a number". In the poem's final stanza, however, he turns all those violated, difficult-to-imagine human numbers into a palpable, carefully handled presence:

> Take me back to my country
> and I can show you the numbers.
> The numbers who suffer.
> The quantities of beauty.
> The fallen flowers.

As Clanchy suggests in her introduction, this willingness to stretch the idiomatic patterns of English might have something to do with the fact that "unlike adults, children can learn another language without an accent". These poems demonstrate, time and again, how these young and intuitive speakers enrich the English language – but also, crucially, how their broader cultural experience can be turned to critique their parochial, largely monoglot new nation.

We should defer, finally, to one of *England*'s contributors, who has already formulated a version of these intersecting arguments – a more complex version, in that it draws upon all the powers of paradox and ambiguity that a poem holds to its advantage over the plain prose statement. 'My Poem' by Tarzina Khatun (16) mobilises a sequence of metaphors that allow the poem to stand for a shifting, potentially infinite array of objects lost through exile: the poem is variously "a plate of hot spicy dahl", "the hot polluted air of the place I lived in" and a "sap that fabricates / a hard dull block of molasses". It exits these beautiful, iterative figures with an abrupt turn that has the air of a 'J'accuse':

> It [my poem] is the young farmers in a watery land
> under the intense heat,
> being wrapped in a cloak of frustration and hunger
> and so
>
> my poem is my country,
> my home country.
> And my country is poor.

These layers of claim and counter-claim are tremendously dense and interwoven. The final stanza starts with a non-metaphor that – in the manner of 'I Don't Remember' by Ismail Akthar – explains the conceit that the poem's imaginative game has hinged on: "my poem is my country", declares the speaker, as if we weren't aware by now. But this momentary over-share swiftly turns into a necessary stepping-stone, a premise leading to a far more complicated conclusion: "And my country is poor." Poor primarily – or literally, at least – because it is economically exploited and underdeveloped, but the syllogistic rhythm of the last three lines usher us to a different, still more troubled reading: my poem is my country; my country is poor; therefore my poem is also poor, perhaps, now, in the transferable sense of 'poor quality'. Any halfway sensitive reader will instantly want to dismiss this interpretation out of hand, though again I would argue that we have to listen for what the poet is really telling us.

With Empsonian wit, Khatun asks us to attend to the interlinked meanings of poverty: the injustice of material poverty that so often determines one's chances of being educated, becoming literate, and writing to a standard (good or 'poor') that is conditioned and privileged by material, cultural wealth. The sting of that final line comes from the realisation that a person who was supposed to be a victim of this situation has articulated, and exploded, it precisely. The reversal is recognisable from postcolonial theory – *The Empire Writes Back* – yet this brilliant, urgent anthology widens its scope to show how the dynamic can apply for young writers as well. In classrooms and beyond, adults so often dominate and instrumentalise children, patronising their achievements as good for what they are, or as spirited imitations of what adults can do. Reading *England*, it is chastening – but endlessly exciting – to see what happens when you listen to children closely, and centre them in the production of their art.

England: Poems from a School, *ed. Kate Clanchy, Picador, £9.99,*
ISBN 9781509886609

Report

POEMS AND PUDDINGS

Alison Brackenbury

> Page one: *Aunt Margaret's Pudding.*
> Take half a pound of flour,
> three ounces lard (or butter), egg,
> milk, sugar, baking powder.
> Spread jam in basin, summer gleam.
> Poke fire! For ninety minutes, steam.
> ('Start')

Is this a poem or a recipe? The answer, I hope, is both (although poems quickly become strangers to the minds that made them). But I do know exactly where this poem came from: a black oilskin notebook, found, after a death, in the drawer of a battered desk, in the kitchen of a Lincolnshire farmworker's small home. The notebook had belonged to my grandmother, Dorothy Eliza Barnes: 'Dot' to her family. When I knew Dot, she was a shepherd's wife. But, as a young woman, she had worked as an Edwardian professional cook. The black book held dozens of her carefully handwritten recipes. One, 'Aunt Margaret's Pudding', became the inspiration for my poetry collection of the same name.

Dorothy Eliza Barnes

I thought about Dot's book for years. Once, terrifyingly, I lost it. When my fingers found it, wedged at the back of the drawer in its old home, the desk, I realised that its survival was as fragile as memory. "Puzzle Pudding, Feather Cake..." whispered an early poem I wrote, after rereading Dot's recipes. Their names often intrigued me: 'Railway Pudding', 'Vinegar Cake'. But their ingredients, like those of her aunt's pudding, seemed surprisingly few and modest.

I began speculating about flour – "Did slick self-raising come too late?" – then discovered myself thinking deeply about Dot's life: "Nor did you have penicillin, / pethidine, or the Welfare State" ('All Change'). The poems arrived in the course of a year: in clumps, like unsieved flour. At first, they were almost clogged by the rich detail of Dot's recipes. Gradually, they explored her life – and our own. The last poems for the book found a sudden expansiveness, as a whole landscape opened up to me: "muddied as love, the Humber rolled / as we climbed Horkstow Hill" ('On Horkstow Hill').

Although I remembered, with tenderness, the wild flowers of that hill, its "small heartsease, at corn's edge", I did not look back with nostalgia. I would not want my grandmother's life. I have seen a photograph from the 1920s in which she looks half-starved. But as I described her ingredients, "strong, workaday, low-cost – / like all the tastes we lost" ('Ingredients'), I felt, fiercely, that her life had values we had lost: a balance of frugality and extraordinary generosity. Dot was feeding her husband and four children on a low wage:

> Yet when strange men tramped round the farms
> to beg for work in '30s storms
> Dot – between her jobs – would pour
>
> sweetened tea for them before
> sending them out in rain well-fed
> on home-cured bacon and white bread.
>
> ('High-class Food')

As I worked on poems in the bitter days after the Brexit vote, I realised that the children to whom Dot gave sweets in the 1960s, as they stood in the cold at the village bus stop, were the son and daughter of a Polish farm worker.

One ingredient in the 'pudding poems' was my growing appreciation of the women in my past. As a child, I was drawn to the glamour of the working lives of the men in Dot's family. My tall grandfather and uncle rattled uphill in a shepherding cart, pulled by a shaggy cob. They spent all day in the open air with their employer's show sheep, and their own boisterous collies. That was where I wanted to be, although I loved Dot, and wolfed down her dark chocolate blancmange and smoky golden pastries at Sunday tea. It has taken me decades to appreciate how remarkable she was. During those decades, some of the skills of the men in her family have become outmoded. My own cooking remains more erratic than skilled. Like most people in this country, I do not need steamed puddings every day. But Dot's sustaining recipes make wonderful food in a crisis, when I still follow her handwritten instructions.

"Softly the mixture dropped" ('Start'). The 'pudding poems' trickled away too, into magazines and websites. They crossed political boundaries, as they became part of the mix both of the *New Statesman* and *The Spectator*. Other editors picked them out, as I would have seized upon the oozing cherries in Dot's fruit cake. I began to realise the deep appeal of the subject I had stumbled upon. Not everybody in Britain smokes, or drinks. But everybody, from every culture, eats. And, however occasionally or unwillingly, most of us need to cook...

One of the most touching aspects of Dot's notebook was cooperation. It was a book of many hands: Dot's tiny script, a fellow cook's scribbled variation on mincemeat, a country neighbour's dashing recipes for homemade wine. This was a surprise, for I had often thought of my grandmother's life as solitary, as the only cook in a dark Nottingham basement, or the woman making dinner, for absent men, in a remote Lincolnshire kitchen. Writing is, physically, immensely more comfortable. But it is also solitary, sometimes lonely.

Dot's recipes brought me an unaccustomed joy: collaboration. Her words from her black notebook found a new home in a small but very special book, *Aunt Margaret's Pudding*, from an independent press, Helena Nelson's HappenStance. I had been struck, as I read through Dot's recipes, how she collected version after version of key recipes like Christmas puddings, comparing, perfecting... Cooking at this level is an art. I do not think that poems can reach perfection, but they do appreciate diligent polishing. It is hard for writers, working in the raw darkness of family history, to view their own poems clearly. Glyn Pursglove, who reviewed *Aunt Margaret's Pudding* in *Acumen*, kindly called the poems "plain and

Puzzle Pudding.

5 tablespoon's flour, 4 of suet 3 of suga
1 teacupful of jam, 1 teaspoonful car-so
Mix with milk Steam 2 hrs.

Cup Pudding.

2 eggs their weight of flour, and sug
the weight of one in butter. 1 teaspoon
B.P. grated lemon rind. Beat the butt
to a cream beat in the sugar and
eggs (well beaten) and flour. B P and ri
Half fill some buttered cups and bake
½ an hour in moderate oven or steam
2½ hrs in buttered basin.

Hamlyppies Pudding Steam 2

The weight of 2 eggs in butter and flour
and half in sugar 3 tablespoonful's
raspberry jam mixed in and a little B. P

Paste for Pork pies.

7 lbs flour. 3 lbs lard. (rubbed in flour
a little salt. Mix with 2 pts boiling
water and milk.

Christmas Puddings (makes 6)
2 lbs breadcrumbs, Suet, Currants,
raisins, 1 lb flour 2 lb. 1 lb sugar 1¼ lbs carrots
10 oz candied peel. 8 eggs. little salt.

Mincemeat.

1½ lbs suet 3 lb raisins. 3 lbs apples
ooked) 3 lbs Currants 2¼ lbs brown sugar, 1 lb Candied
eel. 3 lemons. 1 small nutmeg 1 teaspoon
ace. 1 of ginger. 1 jar marmalade

Christmas Pudding

lb treacle 1 lb raisins 1 lb grated
rrats 1 lb bread crumbs ¾ lb flour
lb course sugar ¼ lemon peel
lb currents 1 lb suet 1 lb apples
ated nut meg & salt

Mincemeat

2 lb Currants 2 lb Apples
2 lb Raisins 2 lb Sugar
¼ lb Peel 3 lemons or 4 oranges
Pinch of Salt.

delicate". The plainness is mine. The delicacy is almost entirely due to Helena's fastidious editing.

This was not a book for a conventional press. Helena agreed that we needed illustrations. Our resident cameraman supplied high-definition images of Dot's steam-smudged recipes, to go with the strangely compelling photograph of her as a young cook, in her Sunday best, with her flowered collar, her neat brooch and her intense, half-anxious gaze.

Helena also suggested that the puddings should be accompanied by a prose account of my grandmother's surprisingly eventful life. Dot had found herself without her mother, who was stung fatally by a bee, before she was two. There were mysteries, too. Dot must have suffered from the general sorrows and hardships of the First World War. But had she also lost someone she loved? Why, on a dark and stormy Lincolnshire evening, did she suddenly speak to me with such urgency of her twentieth year, the summer of 1914: "the loveliest you ever saw"? I can only say that she wanted this summer remembered. I have done my best, in *Aunt Margaret's Pudding*.

The book's final ingredient was a selection of Dot's recipes, original and modernised. How do you translate a "quick fire" into Celsius? Many puddings were steamed: haphazardly by me, methodically by Helena. It was Helena – not me! – who appeared at an Edinburgh reading with a bagful of 'Raspberry Buns', her homemade jam sealed in each perfect sphere. Even our hosts at the Lighthouse Bookshop found their interval brightened by crumble and fruit. Dot would have been proud of her.

I have had poetry published for almost forty years. But I have never had such a wide and warm response as that to *Aunt Margaret's Pudding*. Readers bought extra copies for friends and family, who did not normally read poetry, but devoured Dot's life – and her recipes. They even began to cook. A male friend of mine, who had just taken up cookery, worked his way, with increasing confidence, through every recipe. Dot's own skills were exceptional. Yet, unlike the fantastic confections of some television cooks, her 'Raspberry Buns' and 'Quaker Oat Scones' can be made by almost anyone. Even my poems about Dot, I was told, were consumed by non-poetry readers with relish.

Finally, the 'pudding poems' slipped past the Dalek in the foyer of New Broadcasting House to invade BBC Radio. Their ally and my collaborator was Julian May, an award-winning radio producer with a passion for poetry. In June this year, Radio 4 broadcast a half-hour feature: *What Sweetness Touched Your Tongue?* This included many of my poems, from which the title was taken. But the programme was a triumph of editorial mixing. Like a distant tune, Julian kept a litany of the recipes in the background: 'Paste for Pork Pies', 'Elderberry Syrup', 'Bramble Vinegar'... But the narrative strength of *What Sweetness* came from a blend of many voices. Listeners heard me, reading my favourite poems and telling stories; the actress Emma Handy, narrating Dot's life; and the food historian and demon cook, Dr Annie Gray, whose comments placed Dot in the historical context of her two centuries.

Annie explained how recipes (like poems!) escaped from Victorian printed books into the wider world. With the speed of the true professional, she boiled up a magnificent 'Flamberries Pudding'. This is the pick of Dot's puddings, veined through with luscious (and scaldingly hot) raspberry jam. It was new to Annie – and even she did not know the meaning of Dot's mysterious noun: "Flamberries".

What Sweetness Touched Your Tongue? became an instant critical success. The puddings were chosen as a *Radio Times* Choice, and a 'Radio Pick' in *The Observer*. After broadcast, they appeared again on the menu of BBC Radio 4's *Pick of the Week*. John Waite called *What Sweetness* "mouth-watering". I was especially glad to have poems escape into a second Radio 4 programme, with even wider ripples of response.

It took me two days to answer all the messages on social media, on behalf of the puddings. (I normally find it awkward to discuss my own work. But, strangely, I have always felt it my urgent duty to speak about the poems for Dot, perhaps because, like her notebook, they are the work of many hands.) Some listeners, such as a Lincolnshire craft baker, had particular connections with my grandmother's life and recipes. Others asked about the music I chose for the programme: old Lincolnshire songs, in young and haunting voices. Many women told me that they too had family recipes – scribbled down on old calendars and bills – which they were now determined to keep, bring back to warm life in their own kitchens, and to pass on to their children.

And, finally, I learnt the meaning of 'flamberries'. One helpful listener told me that she had heard the word used by an old gardener, a contemporary of Dot's, who had spent his whole life not in Lincolnshire, but in Gloucestershire (where I now live). It was his word for 'raspberries'. Did it come from the French word 'framboises'? Perhaps, like the old songs I love, it had broken free from print to be remade by the voices of cooks and gardeners. Dot, with this unknown noun, had defeated Google. As

Dr Annie Gray noted, I have now planted 'flamberries' in the wilderness of the web. It seems to me a fine word: a tiny bright piece of salvage. My grandparents were part of a dignified and quiet generation. But they left their own written records of their skills. I think poems may face our dangerous future more strongly if they can salvage what is best from our past.

Dot's notebook and the 'pudding poems' taught me the value of a small subject, approached with love. I will risk one rueful piece of advice, from *Then* (Carcanet, 2013), a collection I published after my parents died: "Ask everything you want to!" I had always lingered at the Sunday tea table to hear the slow stories of the old: of death from sleeping in damp straw at a sheep show, of gunpowder used to clean a kitchen range. But how I wish I had asked my father what songs his father and mother knew! Those songs are gone.

On a more cheerful and seasonal note, I am happy to supply anyone who asks with a list of ingredients I did not mix into my book: the frugal "grated carrot" and the generous "candid peel" of Dot's recipe for Christmas Pudding. It will, of course, make six...

> *Alison Brackenbury,* Aunt Margaret's Pudding, *HappenStance, £8, ISBN 9781910131435*

THE DYING LIGHT

Leonard Cohen, The Flame, *Canongate, £20,*
ISBN 9781786893130

Chris Moss on the last words of Leonard Cohen

...

Leonard Cohen's death in November 2016, at the age of eighty-two, prompted the usual media outpouring that greets the passing of any influential rock or pop music artist. Many obituaries were fawning, a few were perceptive. Cohen's songs, pointed out one critic, seemed polished and pared down unlike those of Dylan – recently anointed a Nobel laureate – which seemed to "pour out" of him. If this is a poetic effect rather than a measure of the craft, it remains a compelling interpretation. Dylan himself said Cohen's songs were "like prayers". Suzanne Vega expanded this to "like prayers or spells".

Writing about death, Cohen was less delicate than his obituarists. His 1956 debut book of poetry, *Let Us Compare Mythologies*, published when he was twenty-two years old, confronts the subject with a young man's rapturous sensuality:

> [...] And do not examine the angry rivers
> For shreds of his soft body
> Or turn the shore stones for his blood;

But in the warm salt ocean
He is descending through cliffs
Of slow green water [...]
('Elegy')

Over the years, he peppered his oeuvre with many songs about mortality. From early reworkings of biblical texts in 'Story of Isaac' and 'Who By Fire' to the looming crescendo of 'Avalanche' – based on an earlier poem – to 1984's graveside hymn 'Night Comes On', he evolved a conversational style of delivery and avoided the typical emotional excesses of threnody. The lyrics of 'You Want It Darker', the title track from his final album, indicate this attitude lasted till the end.

If you are the dealer, I'm out of the game
If you are the healer, it means I'm broken and lame
If thine is the glory then mine must be the shame
You want it darker
We kill the flame.

With his last book, *The Flame*, Leonard Cohen blows out the candle on a career that has been long, wavering, intermittently brilliant. Despite publishing around a dozen poetry collections and two novels, he was never able to commit to words without music. In the foreword, his son, Adam, writes, "My father, before he was anything else, was a poet. He regarded this vocation, as he records in his notebooks, as some 'mission from G–d'." (The dash echoes the Jewish use of the vowel-less YWVH.) Adam claims his father got "high" and found "relief from the suffering" only when writing poems and regretted sacrificing so much of his time to folk song and the fame it brought him.

The sixty-three poems that open the book are combined with lyrics from the four last Cohen albums (three as performer, one as producer and writer), scraps and unfinished verses from his notebooks, and Cohen's drawings and doodles. Themes and motifs recur across the verses and occasional prose pieces: fire and flame imagery; bad love, desperate love; war; exile; America's reckless power and coming apocalypse; booze; Cohen's malign influence over others; the poverty of his poems ("I, a second-rater / by any estimation"); biblical and Jewish allusions; death. Tonally, there's a sombreness that might be called deadbeat, down-at-heel, gloom-laden, but it's usually bone-dry. Cohen, often caricatured as a dirge-writer and wrist-slitter, was too sardonic to be mawkish.

I'm slowing down the tune
I never liked it fast
You want to get there soon
I want to get there last.
('Slow')

Cohen's work displays an attitude to love and desire that is of its time – he was, after all, born in 1934 – yet unashamedly personal.

So I can see your beauty now
Though seeming from afar
Until my neutral world allow
How intimate you are.
('I Didn't Know')

Cohen satirised his 'ladies' man' status on several songs and in the title of a 1977 album; nonetheless, you sense he delights in using poetry as a means to charm his (female) readers. Nothing is as seductive as self-deprecation. He also knew, penning these late poems, that he had the seniority to get away with what might otherwise be viewed as a dated male gaze; to be old fashioned is, carefully managed, to be romantic.

There are other qualities that are more like tonal keynotes. In poems and songs alike, Cohen typically opts for the simplest words and shortest lines, driven along on anapests or iambs towards a clinching rhyme:

In the prison of the gifted
I was friendly with the guard
So I never had to witness
what happens to the heart
('Happens to the Heart')

You tore your knees apart
The loneliness revealed

That drew this unborn heart
From chains that would not yield
('I Didn't Know')

Easy rhythms, a handy prop for songwriting, can feel clumsy and repetitive on the page. It's as if Cohen is leaving space for a horn or a trumpet, or one of his angelic choruses. But it's also as if the brevity is a cage, or a tiredness of spirit.

Or is it that I'm hearing things? When we read Cohen we can't but listen for that famous bass vocal, inimitably deep, as gravelly as that of any legendary smoker (aged eighty, Cohen boasted of returning to the "Parthenon of tobacco"), and supremely, if self-mockingly, ponderous. Poets who practice the more lucrative arts of singing and songwriting can't be blamed for giving their readers accidental music. Even those who are genuine wordsmiths – Cohen and Dylan, for sure, but also Joni Mitchell, Jarvis Cocker, Kate Bush, Morrissey – have such familiar and distinctive timbres that their most casual utterance or chance scribble seems to come vinyl-ready.

On the upside it makes the reader feel they are being talked to by a person rather than a poem or abstract 'writer'. On the down, it overlays the experience with lingering memories of great songs and of the man and the legend, arguably giving the verses a patina of immortality they might not deserve. Only the very famous can print their doodles and unfinished scraps, and *The Flame* has something of the sacred text about it – as if every word the great guru penned is worthy of chanting.

If *The Flame* is uneven and unfinished, that is partly to do with the circumstances of its production. The author was in considerable pain and discomfort as he compiled and tidied up his last offerings. It is when he becomes prayerful, in verses about old friends, loved and lost women, facing sickness and death, his father and mother, that Cohen-poet achieves some of the grandeur of Cohen-singer-songwriter.

'Homage to Morente', one of the longest pieces, in free verse, finds him overwhelmed by admiration for the flamenco singer Enrique Morente: "When I listen to Morente / I know what I must do / When I listen to Morente / I don't know what to do." It's a paradox he returns to time and again: to find in art the impossibility of realising one's art. "I dig but I can't go down."

But through the "mud of hope" and the "blood of the throat" – that is, through the roots music of flamenco and the strains of Morente's cante jondo – Cohen is reaching out to one of his primal poetic influences: Federico García Lorca. We see Lorca's ghost in Cohen's idolects – his juxtapositions of law and love, flags and feelings – and in the way his poems work through refrains and repetitions, as if we're being invited to watch the writing process. The very notion of using art to realise one will always fail as an artist is quintessentially Lorcan.

Cohen requested that *The Flame* include a speech given in Spain in October 2011, when he received the Prince of Asturias Award. He thanks Spain and recalls his first tentative touches of the guitar, guided by a flamenco virtuoso, and expresses his deepest gratitude to Lorca, who "gave me permission to find a voice, to locate a voice; that is, to locate a self, a self that is not fixed, a self that struggles for its own existence."

It is, then, perhaps pointless to revisit the songs-versus-poems debate. Cohen's songs have appeared in his poetry books since 'Suzanne' featured in 1966's *Parasites of Heaven* (probably as a filler). What burns in *The Flame* is an elderly man's last efforts not to contain or summarise the self but to declare the right to keep on searching. The self, like every life, is always an unfinished business, and it's one of poetry's great deceptions to present itself in books, with stiff dustproof covers, and self-important colophons. Cohen, for all the fame and fortune – much of which, anyway, was stolen from him by an unscrupulous manager – evinces more humility than a thousand lesser scribes, and all his love songs have the aching sorrow of failure and truth. He will go down as a romantic of the twentieth century, a troubled troubadour, a truth-seeker who fell back on love, and then got that wrong, too. As he puts it himself, in an untitled, unsung, dateless, unfinished 'poem' towards the end of this final collection:

> I'm standing here
>   in the blinding light
> & I don't know what to do
> the blinding light
>   of what I lost
>
> when I walked away from you

Chris Moss writes on books, travel, art and architecture for various publications.

A PAST THAT WON'T LIE DOWN

Tracy K. Smith, Wade in the Water, *Penguin, £8.99,*
ISBN 9780141987842
August Kleinzahler, Before Dawn on Bluff Road / Hollyhocks in the Fog, *Faber, £14.99,* *ISBN 9780571340361*

Dzifa Benson finds two American poets looking back

. . .

Although these two poets write with different dictions, they both write with a spare lucidity that is plainspoken and deeply attuned to nature and urbanity. This is where their similarities, at least on the surface, end. Kleinzahler is white, an elder statesman of American poetry and two decades older than Smith, who is female, black and the incumbent US Poet Laureate. While Kleinzahler's consideration of people is filtered through the poet's own internal mapping, Smith's poetry is more expansively empathetic across time and space. If Kleinzahler can be described as a poet of place then Smith is a poet of people.

The title of Smith's fourth collection, *Wade in the Water*, trails a lot of associative freight even before you've opened the book. If you know the melody and lyrics of the song of the same title, the tune is likely to pervade your reading of the collection. Having started as a spiritual associated with the Underground Railroad (which smuggled slaves to liberty and safety in nineteenth-century America) it's become a blues/jazz standard and has been covered by or inspired artists as various as Nick Cave, Bob Dylan, Marlena Shaw, Cerys Matthews, The Staple Singers, The Ramsey Lewis Trio and Fine Young Cannibals. The song's roots in protest (its biblical references to the Israelites' escape from Egypt were also apparently code to help slaves escape) lend this – a poetic cover version? – even deeper layers of meaning in the way Smith has yoked the past to the present.

The biblical allusions and weighty subject matter don't end there in this book, which serves as a commentary on America's problematic history, its fraught current moment and uncertain future. The very first poem, 'Garden of Eden', with its references to fruit that have the word 'apple' in their etymology and the implicit idea that there is something poisonous here, starts with a moment of self-recognition for the speaker:

> Everyone I knew was living
> The same desolate luxury,
> Each ashamed of the same things:
> Innocence and privacy.

There's shame in this privileged retreat to a false innocence and sense of self-containment in the face of the ills that plague America. This is a more terrestrially rooted collection than Smith's previous one, the Pulitzer Prize-winning *Life on Mars* (2011), with its cosmological enquiry, which also served as an elegy to her father. Since her appointment as laureate in 2017, Smith has travelled to small, rural communities across the States, in a project she sees as a kind of literary evangelism. It's evident that the poet has used this collection as a further platform to bear witness to historical and current racial, gender, social and environmental injustice – "a past / that's gone but won't lie down / And let us grieve it" ('Driving to Ottawa'). It's a world where God himself, in the poem 'Hill Country', desires something larger than himself to rearrange the air.

Such fervour lends the collection a proselytising edge, compelling the reader to step out of her "desolate luxury" and empathise with someone unknown. It's very present in the poem that is the linchpin of the collection, 'I Will Tell You the Truth About This, I Will Tell You All About It', in which Smith manipulates letters written during the Civil War by African Americans (leaving misspellings and grammatical mistakes intact) – soldiers begging for their pensions, wives pleading to see their spouses and mothers asking to see their only children. This is the nearest thing to hearing the subjects' own voices and all the more moving for that.

If we take the speaker in 'Watershed', a poem about environmental atrocities, to represent the poet herself, then these lines can be interpreted as the key to the poet's intentions for this book: "a great / opportunity to use my background for people who / really needed it". However, a lot of 'Watershed' feels more like reportage presented as poetry, which dilutes the impact of the book as a whole, fighting as it does against the form and diction that makes a piece of writing a poem, lineated or not. Even so, it aligns with the theme of compassion that runs throughout the book. In the end, the collection repeatedly tends towards love – which is directly mentioned in so many poems – as a transformative force. In 'Unrest in Baton Rouge', Smith contemplates Jonathan Bachman's iconic photograph of Ieshia Evans in a billowing black-and-white sundress protesting the death of Alton Sterling and squaring up to armoured police:

> Is it strange to say love is a language
> Few practice, but all, or near all speak?
>
> Even the men in black armor, the ones
> Jangling handcuffs and keys, what else
>
> Are they so buffered against, if not love's blade
> Sizing up the heart's familiar meat?

And in 'Watershed': "*Viewing the myriad human faces with an incredible, intimate, and profound love. This love was all around me, it was everywhere, but at the same time it was also me.*"

This continuous push to find connection is a trope that Smith employs in the poem 'Eternity': "Every chance I get, every face I see, I find myself / Searching for a glimpse of myself, my daughter, my sons". Uncannily, this is mirrored in Kleinzahler's poem 'Self-Portrait' from *Before Dawn on Bluff Road: Selected New Jersey Poems*:

> filled to bursting, commuters illuminated,
> each face vivid, highlighted—is that you?—
> exasperation, fatigue, concern at the time.

However, Kleinzahler's image is determinedly and balefully directed inwards. In fact, this whole selection (which Faber has published tête-bêche alongside *Hollyhocks in the Fog: Selected San Francisco Poems*) is suffused with a creeping melancholia that is more than hinted at at the end of the first and title poem: "I remember / almost nothing of my life". It is made explicit a few poems later in 'Family Album': "Loneliness—huge, suddenly menacing / and no one is left here who knows me anymore". It takes on the flavour of mortal angst in 'Portrait of My Mother in January':

> Afternoons are the most difficult.
> They seem to have no end,
> no end and no one there.
> Outside the trees do their witchy dance.
> Mother grows smaller in her chair.

In 'Blue at Four P.M.' it is transformed into heady, gorgeous language and surprising imagery:

> The burnish of late afternoons
> as winter ends—
> this sadness coming on in waves in not round
> and sweet
> as the doleful cello
>
> but jagged, intent
> finding out places to get through the way the wind
> tries seams
> and cracks in the old house, making
> the furnace kick on

Where there is an urgency to Smith's poetry, Kleinzahler's has a cool and considered watchfulness. He has said in an interview: "When I was younger, it wasn't unusual for me to have 50, 100, 200 drafts of a poem." That care makes for poetry that must be read with all senses alert to rhythm and sound associations that reveal themselves with attentive reading. There is subtle music here. Despite the poet's precision, there is a lightness of touch to the work that lends it a freewheeling, spontaneous quality. This is a poet who is alive to everything and all those drafts must help to boil a theme down to its essence.

Peripateticism informs Kleinzahler's poetry more than anything else. This isn't just travelling from place to place, it's also a journeying through time, seasons and neighbourhoods where the speaker knows the names of shopkeepers and residents. This inquisitiveness about people sits in curious tension with the poems' proclamations of loneliness. Not only is the poet fascinated by going to places, he is also intrigued by where things are coming from. In a poem like 'Sunday Nocturne', for example, planes arrive from Dakar, Akron, Samoa and "A gentleman // in Italian loafers / disembarks". Even a poem about a sleeping cat, 'Cat in Late Autumn', still manages to incorporate "olive oil cans from Lucca and the groves / near Córdoba".

The later collection of Kleinzahler poems within this volume, *Hollyhocks in the Fog: Selected San Francisco Poems*, feels even more precise in its use of language. If the New Jersey Palisades overshadow *Before Dawn on Bluff Road* then fog is the rule for *Hollyhocks*. It's as if the poet has to be more exacting with language in order to 'see' and write through the actual and metaphorical fog. These poems are sparer, grittier than the New Jersey poems, with a cynical edge. The speaker of most of the poems here sounds regretfully and resentfully older. That Scrooge-like acridity reveals itself in poems like 'Watching a Young Couple with an Old Girlfriend on Sunday Morning' and 'Ebenezer Californicus', a poem as ungenerously misanthropic as its name suggests. There is a poignancy lacing through the bitterness. In 'Late Indian Summer':

> Nights already belong to winter.
> You know by that tuning fork in its jacket
> of bone
> broadcasting to the body's far ports.

This suggests the poet is acutely aware that he has more years behind than ahead of him. As such, this double volume, collecting poems from two geographical fulcrums of the poet's life, is very timely indeed.

Dzifa Benson is a poet, dramatist and performance artist based in London.

MY LIFE AND YOUR LIFE

Eve L. Ewing, Electric Arches, *Haymarket, $16,*
ISBN 9781608468560
Raymond Antrobus, The Perseverance, *Penned in the Margins,*
£9.99, ISBN 9781908058522
Fiona Moore, The Distal Point, *HappenStance, £10,*
ISBN 9781910131442

Sarala Estruch encounters true stories, dramatic monologues and medicine for grief

. . .

In the note of introduction to her debut collection, *Electric Arches*, writer, scholar, artist and sociologist Eve L. Ewing writes, "This book is about my life and maybe also your life. And it is about the places we invent. Every story in it is absolutely true." Hence we are immediately introduced to the work's preoccupations with the transformative and unifying powers of language and the imagination, as well as its probing exploration of what constitutes 'truth', 'story' and, above all, 'history'. "Everybody has a history, every institution has a history, every neighborhood, every rock, tree and car," said Ewing in a recent interview with the *New York Times*. But in mainstream society, certain histories are privileged while many more are silenced. *Electric Arches* is concerned with giving voice to the personal and collective stories of black girlhood and womanhood, and the challenges and possibilities of growing up as a black girl in contemporary America, specifically Chicago.

The work is framed by two poems which are dedicated to Assata Shakur, a member of the Black Liberation Army who was convicted (many believe wrongly) of the murder of a white police officer in 1977 but who escaped from prison in 1979 and was granted political asylum in Cuba where she lives to this day. The opening poem, 'Arrival Day', is a speculative poem which describes, in energetic and original verse, black revolutionaries as aliens who "under cover of night or early morning" "drop from the moon" and arrive in modern-day Chicago. It is a highly imaginative, innovative and vibrant poem delivered with a lightness of tone and humour which make the underlying racial tensions all the more resonant and painful, particularly when the poem returns, abruptly, from its imaginative heights back to everyday reality:

> [...] the boy down the street, who in smaller days I walked
> to school when his mother worked early, who loved lime
> popsicles the best [...]
> [...] who the police had recently declared a man, stopping
> him mid-two-step to ask questions he could not answer because the
>   query beneath
> them was "why are you alive"

The closing poem, 'Affirmation', is dedicated to "youth living in prison" and is one of Ewing's more hopeful and life-affirming poems: "Put a finger to my wrist or my temple / and feel it: I am magic". Ewing's poems are frequently celebratory, often taking commonplace items and eulogising them as emblematic of the black female experience (such as 'Shea Butter Manifesto' and 'Ode to Luster's Pink Oil') although, as in 'Arrival Day', the darkness of racial prejudice always lurks just beyond the page.

Her use of form is as innovative as her ideas and images are original. The collection includes visual art, speculative poems, short stories, retellings of personal encounters with racism (reminiscent of Claudia Rankine's *Citizen*, but which progress into wildly imaginative – and often hilarious – speculative endings that have been added in Ewing's handwriting), even a sonnet consisting of a single line repeated fourteen times which reveals the tenderness behind the simple but thoughtful action "I saved some cornbread for you in the skillet on the oven" ('sonnet').

Raymond Antrobus's *The Perseverance* is also both highly personal and political. Like Ewing, Antrobus is adept at conveying the current climate of racial and class tensions, although the primary settings here are England and Jamaica. If Ewing's collection can be described as a paean to black girlhood and womanhood in Chicago, *The Perseverance* can be described as a moving account of a D/deaf, mixed-race boy's journey to manhood. However, the collection is far more than a straightforward work of autobiography; it is a tightly wrought body of poetry, which poignantly probes the challenges and possibilities of D/deaf identity, mixed-race identity and modern-day masculinity.

In his pamphlet, *To Sweeten Bitter*, Antrobus wrote movingly about negotiating his Jamaican British heritage and his relationship with his late father. In this full collection, the poet continues to explore questions of identity and belonging in a postcolonial world. In 'Aunt Beryl Meets Castro', the speaker declares that "Castro, / him understan' the history / of dem who harm us, who / make the Caribbean a / kind of mix up mix up / pain", and in 'Miami Airport', racist prejudices combine with stereotypes of D/deafness when the security guard refuses to believe that the poet is either British ("why didn't I see anyone that looked like you / when I was in England?") or deaf ("you don't look deaf?)". Where the collection goes further, however, is in its broader and deeper exploration of the D/deaf experience. The opening poem, 'Echo' is a tour de force in which plosives and sibilant sounds abound, conveying the experience of using hearing aids:

> My ear amps whistle as if singing
> to Echo, Goddess of Noise,
> the ravelled knot of tongues,
> of blaring birds, consonant crumbs
> of dull doorbells, sounds swamped
> in my misty hearing aid tubes.

Many of the poems are dramatic monologues through which D/deaf individuals are given space to share their stories, from the artist in 'Conversation with the Art Teacher (A Translation Attempt)' to the historical figure of Mabel Bell, wife of Alexander Graham Bell, in 'The Shame of Mable Gardiner Hubbards'.

The Perseverance also reads as an elegy to the poet's late father, exploring as it does their relationship, as well as the father's relationship to the poet's deafness. The final poem, 'Happy Birthday Moon', is a deeply moving pantoum in which the young poet and his father are reading together from a children's book and, through their various attempts, they learn to laugh at their struggles and in so doing begin to "hear each other, really hear each other".

Fiona Moore's *The Distal Point* is another collection concerned with language's ability – or, at times, inability – to appease human suffering. In 'The Only Reason For Time Is So That Everything Doesn't Happen At Once', the speaker states "I will get language where I can" as if it is a medicine for grief but one that is hard to procure.

The title itself comprises an anatomical and geographical term which means "situated away from the centre of the body or an area or from the point of attachment" (OED). In the opening section of the book, the title appears to relate to the poet who has lost her "point of attachment" in the form of her spouse/life partner who, we infer, died of cancer. The poems in this section are tightly controlled, acting both as vessel for and release of the grief that so completely suffuses them. These are meditations on the nature of time, which grief transforms into something "that is not linear as it seemed" ('The Only Reason For Time Is So That Everything Doesn't Happen At Once'), as well as the nature of change "that's slow, and slow, and one day total" ('Island').

In the second section of the book, we are offered a more literal definition of "the distal point" in a poem titled 'Exclave', in which Moore uses West Berlin as a metaphor for something approaching a state of transition, and which seems to be applicable to experiences as wide-ranging as death or leaving the European Union:

> We drove to the frontier once, or as far as we could:
>   [...] We looked
> into silence: the trees and fields empty of
> barbed wire, a mine strip, high guard towers
> with a gate, if any, only to be opened
> at the end of the world as we knew it.

The second section engages most directly with politics and history, and includes a poem which describes how prisoners were hung from meat-hooks in Plötzensee Prison, another which evokes the anti-austerity riots in Greece and another that details a discussion of Wall's Neapolitan ice cream, and which poses timely questions about how differences can be preserved within a unified whole.

In the third and final section, Moore returns to poems of love and loss, but with a voice that is less grief-stricken, more assured. Here, the poems are less constrained by form. It is as if the grief, having quieted to a gentle ache rather than an all-engulfing wound, can now be given more space, more freedom, and, as a result, vestiges of hope begin to appear. In the final poem, 'To the Moon', it is as if the poet can now take pleasure in striving for the unknown and the unattainable – she can joyfully inhabit the distal point:

> Moon, here's a heart
> in the sand, and over there a lantern launched
>
> straight for you, a circle of orange flame
> soaring towards
> destruction: the higher, the more complete.

Sarala Estruch a London-based writer, poet and Ledbury Emerging Poetry Critic.

ANYTHING THAT BURNS

Lola Ridge, To the Many: Collected Early Works, *Little Island, £14.99,* *ISBN 9780993505645*

Rio Matchett on a neglected modernist

...

To *the Many* collects the early poetry of Lola Ridge, from 1919–1927, alongside the previously unpublished *Verses*, written sometime around 1905. Born Rose Emily in Dublin in 1873, Ridge emigrated to New Zealand at the age of three with her mother. From there she absconded to Australia to attend art school, and at the age of thirty-three ran away to California with her son. She would leave him there and head to New York, having shaved ten years off her age and omitted her husband from her immigration papers – the name 'Lola' is one she adopted. Hugely influential in her own time, both as a poet and an editor, Ridge is a nexus of contradiction: the waif-like, ephemeral poet who was the last to stand her ground in front of a rearing police horse; the starving bohemian who managed to acquire tickets to California, New York, Mexico and Baghdad; the voice of working America, who with multiple migrations and an anti-state agenda, was a citizen of nowhere; the spokesperson for the Jewish immigrant community, with no discernible Jewish heritage.

Daniel Tobin's editorial of the book offers unprecedented juxtapositions of Ridge's early work, which allow for many fruitful new readings and comparisons. As tempting as it is to want to piece together Ridge's identity from her poems, the true merit of this collection lies not in revealing hers, but ours. For some reason, interest has come back to her. We rewrite history as it suits us to reflect the present, and the resurgence of interest in Lola Ridge has plenty to tell us about how we see ourselves, how we see transnationalism, and how we conceive of our own identities, one hundred years on from her first collection's publication. Her work leads us to ask how and whether we can ever become our own constructs. Can we truly abandon motherhood, nationality, age? Her work speaks to choice, to women's choice, and to democratic choice. Potential bubbles throughout the work – in 'Submerged', she writes:

> Oh, could I now dive
> Into the unexplored deeps of me
> Delve and bring up and give
> All that is submerged, encased, unfolded
> That is yet the best.

A kind of pyromania runs through the collection. Cleansing, destructive, warming and life-giving by turn, the image of fire is present in the vast majority of her verses. Ridge burned up her identity – and her past – with the same fire that permeates her poetry, leaving her the freedom to truly reconstruct her own sense of self in the present moment. This elusive identity, not least coupled with her radical politics, has left Ridge's work largely forgotten until recent years. The pendulum of American interest swung far from the radical left after the Second World War, with the rise of McCarthyism and the Red Scare, and the unavoidable ghost of gender floats above Ridge's lost legacy. Although she was an editor for influential magazines *Broom* and *Others*, Ridge was all but edited out of the history of modernist, political and women poets. From the 1927 collection *Red Flag*, an extract from Ridge's poem 'Russian Women' epitomises her socialism, her feminism, her anarchism and her fervent style:

> In you unimagined circuits,
> in you uncoiled
> passion electric –
> the stroke swift
> and the recoil as swift [...]
> in you the unidentified power –

hysteria directed,
the world force.

Red Flag is imbued with the Russian anarchist influence Ridge had absorbed over the 1920s, and the fiery imagery is typical of her work:

Red light burning down the centuries
Red fire dwindling to a spark but never out
[...] Red flag over the domes of Moscow.

A citizen of nowhere is, by extraction, a citizen of everywhere, and Ridge's radical politics are perhaps the thing for which she is best remembered. When asked in an interview what was the proper subject for poetry, Ridge replied "anything that burns you". The injustice of class and gender hegemonies were clearly two of her greater bugbears, with her class politics born out most clearly in her first and third collections, *The Ghetto* (1918) and *Red Flag*. *The Ghetto* moves from Imagist visions of East New York, through calls to socialist arms before somewhat awkwardly tracking back to nature. These are among the least successful of her poems, with phrases such as "The naked soul in the sunlight... / Like a wisp of smoke in the sunlight / On the hill-side shimmering" ('Dispossessed') feeling a little naive when compared to Ridge's more impassioned political work.

A notable moment in this collection is Tobin's juxtaposition of Ridge's poetry with her 1919 essay 'Woman and the Creative Will', an adapted speech which challenged the limitations of women's creativity some ten years before Virginia Woolf's *A Room of One's Own*. This fascinating essay takes a problematically essentialist view of gender, and draws intense parallels between the "uneducated worker of the world" and the suppressed woman; both, Ridge declares, have a genuine but acquired inferiority. In this essay we see a bold and intelligent woman, wrestling with the received wisdom of her time, and emerging not without flaw, but certainly with vigour.

With the privilege of hindsight, the onus must lie with the reader to separate the good will of the poet from a problematic method. Though she was hailed in her lifetime as a voice defending the impoverished Jewish immigrants of the Lower East Side, Ridge's description in *The Ghetto* of a Jewish merchant, whose "thrifty eyes / Bend – glittering, intent / Their hoarding looks / Upon his merchandise" ('The Ghetto') ring sourly in the contemporary ear. In her experiments with voice too, Ridge is difficult. In 'Lullaby', she paints the true story of an incident of the East St Louis race riots, in which a white woman flung a living black baby into the blazing fire. Adopting a pattern of speech that smacks more than a little of Uncle Tom, Ridge's poem is a disturbing and macabre nursery rhyme –

> An' the singin' flame an' the gleeful crowd
> Circlin' aroun'... won't mammy be proud!
> With a stone at her head an' a stone on her heart
> An' her mouth like a red plum, broken apart...

Whilst Ridge's attempts to embody the voices around her are not always fully realised, the most successful poem in the collection, 'Sun Up', is one in which she adopts another voice, that of her younger self. This lengthy autobiographical verse depicts her childhood, growing up in poverty as an outsider in New Zealand where "God throws hailstones", and is bursting with the righteous anger and painful verve of a child – "Mama's eyes stare out of the pillow / as though she had gone away [...] / and you scream at her face". In it, Ridge vividly paints the growing consciousness of youth, questioning whether a child may be violent and yet not bad, whether a person can be great and yet not good. Most ardent in this poem is the combative relationship Ridge explores with God – the tension between her Irish Catholic background, her childhood experiences of abuse and maternal depression, the almost pagan experiences of spirituality she finds in New Zealand as nature becomes her only retreat. Nature is, indeed, the main focus of the previously unpublished *Verses*.

There is always something seductive about early and unpublished work, especially from a writer whose identity is so elusive, and perhaps this expectation is unfair. We want to peer behind the curtain of Ridge's contrived identity, to see who she was before she changed her name, her age, her nationality and marital status. *Verses* then, is unavoidably disappointing, as no such reveal is made – rather, we are subjected to Ridge's most nascent and least original work, including the inevitably romantic: "Let not the thought of me, love, / Be one to bring you pain" ('Think Of Me Not With Sadness'). Demonstrably vital for Ridge's artistic development, her unpublished poems are pleasant at best, and lacking the fire of her later work. This fire – "like flame at an asbestos curtain", "forking-flame", "the white flares of Broadway", "brief fire", "fashioned in fire", "spirals of fire", "vomiting fire" – synchronises Ridge's spirituality with her politics, and creates a vivid through-line to her later work.

In her *New York Times* obituary, Ridge was hailed as one of the most important poets of her time. Her poetry itself ranges from awkward sonnets to brilliant free verse, just as her life, her politics and her legacy evade neat description. In reflection on her own oeuvre, Ridge commented that "Nice is the one adjective in the world that is laughable applied to any single thing I have ever written". Her verdict is fair – the work is not nice or without problem, but it is bursting with life, important, and burning. This collection will, with any luck, stimulate the wider readership that Ridge deserves.

Rio Matchett is a PhD researcher and dramaturg from Liverpool.

STILL RUNNING

Mark Ford, Enter, Fleeing, *Faber, £10.99, ISBN 9780571339990*
Fred D'Aguiar, Translations from Memory, *Carcanet, £12.99, ISBN 9781784106065*

Tim Dooley considers recollections, re-presentations and literary antecedents

. . .

The title of Mark Ford's fourth collection, *Enter, Fleeing*, works well as a pointer to the book's contents. If it suggests wit, anxiety and a kinetic propulsion, what follows does not disappoint. 'Under the Lime Trees' opens with a cyclist alert to dangers from glittering splinters or pedestrians caught up in music. The poem hurtles down the page, swerving through lines of varied length past risky enjambments, while the cyclist races on in his thoughts – conscious now of microscopic threats ("the germ we inhale, unknowing, / and cannot spit out"), now of the body's heroic powers of resistance ("every / active capillary, if challenged, or opposed, or howsoever / aroused, dilates / in bold defiance") – until, parenthesised between two blinks at the sun, a fall arrives:

> ... blink
> again and the fanatical

> flow of money
> and data bursts like a blood vessel, scattering
> the crowds gathered beneath the weeping
> limes.

'Under the Lime Trees' is pointedly contemporary with its allusion to the financial crash and mentions of 'Boris Bikes', yet it's rooted in older traditions. Its title references Walther von der Vogelweide's 'Unter den Linden' (memorably translated by the poet's namesake Ford Madox Ford as 'Tandaradei'). Passing the city's "deserving / poor", the cyclist recalls "Wolves / living on wind" from François Villon's 'Le Lais', or perhaps via Ezra Pound's 'Villonaud for this Yule'.

The subverted literariness of Mark Ford's writing announces itself equally in 'Viewless Wings', a rewriting of Keats's 'Nightingale' ode as an avian bloodbath, and in 'Aloft', which repurposes Baudelaire's 'Le Port' (from *Paris Spleen*) as part of a paean to air travel. That poem's conclusion takes us in a different direction:

> Where are – I mean what happened to – my Junior
> Jet Club Logbook and my framed
> certificates awarded for having flown
> 25,000 miles – 50,000 miles –
> 75,000 miles – 100,000 miles –
> after which we gave up counting
> or they ran out of certificates?

Scattered through *Enter, Fleeing* are minimalist recollections of a childhood spent in Kenya, Nigeria, the USA, Sri Lanka, Hong Kong and the Gulf (dated from 1963 to 1977). The child in these poems is entering a world that is itself in flight: the dog-end of colonialism, with its brittle sense of superiority:

> '*Wait here!*' my mother commanded, white
> with fury; then she set off in pursuit.
>
> [...]
>
> I guess she caught up with the robber, and wrestled
> the bag back, vehemently

demanding, '*How dare you! – How*
DARE you! –

How dare you!'
('Lagos, 1967')

Ford gives us a laconic child's-eye view of the assumed privilege in this micro-society where servants are given English names and face summary dismissal for interruptions to decorum. But he also shows us the fragility of an 'Empire' that is "flummoxed, and dissolving / fast" ('World Enough'). What we see of the English side of an expatriate childhood is equally unnerving, its boarding schools staffed with "some quite creepy men" ('In Loco Parentis'). Many of the adult narrators in *Enter, Fleeing* are also caught up in threatening situations: a mugging in 'Show Time', doping and theft in 'Mickey Finn' and, in 'Fides et Literis' (the poem takes its title from the motto of St Paul's School), fear "that a mad surgeon, needle / and scalpel poised, is on my tail".

The title of Ford's collection is given context by an epigraph from Walter Benjamin's 'One Way Street', where "enter, fleeing" is identified as a stage instruction in plays by Calderón and Shakespeare. Its effect on the performer is such that "[t]he moment in which they become visible to spectators brings them to a standstill". Just so, Ford's protagonists seem caught in the headlights of contemporary experience, startled and uncertain where to run. Ford has found a particularly resonant metaphor for our times.

There are surprising parallels between the careers of Fred D'Aguiar and Mark Ford. Each was born early in the 1960s and had a childhood split between the UK and the tropical South. Both are now professors as well as poets: Ford at UCL, D'Aguiar at UCLA. The difference, of course, is in the route travelled by each poet to reach his current position. D'Aguiar was born in London, but taken back to his parents' home in Guyana for his early childhood, before returning to London for his secondary education and training as a psychiatric nurse. In the glimpses of childhood scattered through his seventh collection, *Translations from Memory*, there are games of hopscotch on "squares drawn in sand" ('Dante'), but also an 'Unofficial Lido', where teenagers "swam in the river / at Deptford / beside Pepys estate".

D'Aguiar went to university as a mature student and his early success as a poet, with *Mama Dot* (1985), led to the unusual situation that before he had graduated his work was already on course reading lists. The contents page of *Translations from Memory* could be read as a particularly exhaustive outline for a higher education course, ranging as it does from 'Museum Gilgamesh', via 'Socrates Plato Aristotle' and 'Hume Meet Locke' to 'DW' (Derek Walcott) and 'KB' (Kamau Brathwaite). Both learned and mischievous, D'Aguiar's new collection revisits the canon, interrogates it and reorganises it. Sometimes his titles lead on to abstract ruminations:

> There is nothing to say that the gods do not
> exist or that they do, yet they may take exception,
> in fact do, to your devotion to another living thing,
> my point, since lightning must strike you, live your life.
> ('Protagoras')

Some, like 'Wilson Harris' or 'Anna Akhmatova', are followed by more or less straightforward tributes, while others play on word association. Plato, for example:

> Is not to be confused with potato,
> though both have skins that a lash might peel
> and a stroke of love might heal.
>
> Is not to be confused with plate
> near empty for the hungry
> brimful for the rich.
> ('Socrates Plato Aristotle')

The appearance of "a lash" here points to the major intervention in D'Aguiar's account of cultural history. Halfway through the collection, in 'Kant', the speaker asks: "Is every damn thing / going to be measured / against old man fat lady slavery?" The answer ("No / yes / hell yes / maybe") is tempered with anxiety, but the considerable achievement of *Translations from Memory* is in representing Western cultural history through the lens of black experience. In classical statuary we see "slaves under / laden tables, who bare teeth, force / smiles" ('Greek & Latin'). Pushkin's "dark skin" is compared to a drum-skin "stretched over wood for bone / tight so that insults bounce off".

As well as finding a black presence that the historical record has obscured, D'Aguiar brings examples of black achievement to centre stage.

Two authors of slavery narratives have poems; 'Equiano' is remembered for "making tea for two volatile" in eighteenth-century England, and 'Douglass' '[f]or sniffing out / Change in unlikely places". There are tributes to thinkers and activists such as C.L.R. James, Martin Carter and Walter Rodney and to key figures in Caribbean literature. D'Aguiar registers change through the action of such figures, "[t]hat made the map lose its focus. / Mercator changed to Peter's" ('Martin Carter'). In the final stanza of the book, however, we are reminded that, despite their achievement (and one might add the achievement of the poet himself), much has remained the same:

> Uniformed guards trail me
> At boutique malls
> I breathe shallow
> Square my shoulders
> Against their hunch
> Align my spine
> With history lived below
> Deck as much as above

The game of hopscotch in 'Dante' enacts the difficulties of progress: "the legs burn from covering // so much ground on one foot, / advancing one square at a time, / from the bottom up". In 'MLK intro', black history becomes a "non-stop treadmill / bound for glory", where W.E.B. Du Bois, Malcolm X and Martin Luther King are imagined as a relay team:

> in a race
> with no finish line, no end in sight, trusting someone will be there
> without your need to say, take my outstretched hand before
> both of us tumble and fail not just ourselves but all who follow us.

This ambitious book shows Fred D'Aguiar still determined to keep running and to look ahead.

Tim Dooley's Weemoed *(Eyewear, 2017) was a Poetry Book Society Recommendation.*

IF THE ENEMY CHOSE

Ellen Hinsey, The Illegal Age, *Arc, £10.99, ISBN 9781911469377*
J.O. Morgan, Assurances, *Cape, £10, ISBN 9781787330856*

Karen McCarthy Woolf reads two long poems exploring power, politics and threat

...

Reading Ellen Hinsey's book-length poem *The Illegal Age* is a bit like stumbling on a secret intelligence dossier mislaid by an absentminded mandarin on the Bakerloo Line. I draw this comparison not only because its structures and language both announce and mimic the formalities of a legal document presented before an international tribunal, but also as its critique of the accelerating erosion of our global democracies is tense and breathtaking. There is something deeply intimate yet expansively wide-ranging in theme and scope, achieved through an adroit blend of lyric and factual expression.

Divided into three parts or 'Investigation Files', consecutively titled 'Smoke', 'Ice' and 'Obscurity', the book opens with a 'Report' (prologue) which reveals the extent of Hinsey's formal ambitions. "Nothing happens quickly" is the opening phrase, and one which is repeated and italicised for emphasis on the following line: a refrain that sets up the temporal framing throughout. The reader is encouraged to take the long view, where history and philosophy intermingle with a spiritual, and at times biblical, register. Yet there is also a note of urgent, (pre-)apocalyptic warning (eg 'Testimony: VII. The Four Horsemen. Warsaw 1944') underscored by a razor-sharp enjambment in each of the following six verses: suggesting that although gradual, the impacts of a resurgence in totalitarian regimes and democratic decline will be (and are) seismic.

> It takes time for a figure, who makes his slow way along
> The foggy lane in innocence, to vanish – for tables
>
> II.
> Laid with silver – for the simple woollen hat twisted
> In rough hands when prayers are said. It takes time
>
> To not suffer the pain of others – to not hope for just
> Mercy. *Nothing happens quickly* – the ravaged book
>
> Of the ancestors remains open – rustles – *persists* –
> ('Part One. Investigation File. Smoke. The Illegal Age')

Carolyn Forché, whose 1993 anthology *Against Forgetting: Twentieth-Century Poetry of Witness* was a landmark text, writes in her introduction to that volume of how a poem may exist as the "only evidence that an event has occurred". In an algorithmic era of fake news, political manipulation and moral disquiet, *The Illegal Age* reiterates this maxim for the twenty-first century, extending it (as an act of persistence) to connect the brutalities and traumas of the First and Second World Wars to present-day human-rights infringements and state-sanctioned violence.

Hinsey is a US poet, essayist and translator, who has lived in Europe for the past two decades. These biographical details are apparent in the book's geographies and affiliations, which exist somewhat independently of a more postcolonial and culturally diverse remit (consider Claudia Rankine's *Citizen* by comparison). Instead, Hinsey's systemic ventriloquisms and theoretical critique trace an outline that snakes forwards from German concentration camps and Russian gulags to an unnamed geopolitical presence, reminiscent of contemporary America. It should also be noted that the book was written over an eight-year period and preceded the current US administration: an important point given its chronological sweep reaching back to ancient Greece and Rome. The book also contains a 'Notes' section at the back, which expands the poems to reveal the book's ideological and literary godparents (Miłosz, Arendt, Celan, Szymborska, Bachmann, Mandelstam), and their associated locales.

In the first of two 'Internal Reports' (within sections marked 'Confidential Document'), a critical analysis of 'The Inconceivable' as an anthropomorphised political concept is chilling, not only for its performative and stark indifference through moments of '*Genesis*', '*Methodology*' and '*Ownership*', but also via point of view. Here, responses to a series of subheadings hint at a more sinister, anonymous authorial voice – where we hear the thoughts and strategies of the puppet masters themselves. The Inconceivable "first merges along the periphery – discreetly agitating on the edges of local chaos"; it bides its time, "mastering territory" until "what stood at the periphery attains the centre", eventually gaining "access to the human heart". After all, this same voice reasons, "One poor person, more or less, will not trouble the sleep of the burghers."

Many of these statements have an aphoristic quality, and the use of imagistic, metaphorical language is elegantly integrated with more overt political assertions, where "disappearances" are compared to "the sudden vanishing of a ragged-winged bird over the far horizon" and 'Power' becomes both concept and character, for whom 'Humility' is "like the modest sheen of wheat that rises in beneficent summer light" ('Internal Report: On the Intimate Daybook of Power'). In part six of that poem there is a section entitled '*The Turn*', which inevitably evokes the sonnet and marks a shift in attitude and tone. At this point "Power" "devours itself like climbing ivy / exhausting a decayed trunk's girth" and "looks pathetic in old age", "affirming a show of masculine force".

The book concludes with a '*Testimony*: On the Progress of History' in which the discipline's "heroics" are deemed "unappreciated", its luggage ditched and "Truth's green branch is twisted" in its "dark knoll". Above all, Hinsey declares, finally, in an appropriately ambivalent passive tense, "History, it has been reported, is tired."

If *The Illegal Age* reads like *Guernica* in its sense of scale and scope, then J.O. Morgan's *Assurances* narrows its focus as a detail rather than a grand canvas. That's not to say that its ambitions are any less expansive as a book-length poem that takes war, and specifically, the technology of war, as its subject. What makes it intimate, tonally and in terms of content, is a biographical provenance that connects it to memoir, the context of which foregrounds the work itself.

Apparently the poet's father was an RAF officer, whose job it was to maintain the "*Airborne Nuclear Deterrent*", during the "early years of the Cold War", and the poem is a representation of what he has gleaned of his father's role during that period. It is a useful and necessary preface, as these details are not easily discernible within the text itself. Without it, there could be moments where a fruitful disorientation that occurs via multiple layers of lyric immersion dissolved the poem's mesmeric vitality.

The narrative commences with a series of syntactically disrupted tercets:

> Born from a need to counteract the threat.
> Now that such a threat.
> For threats have been made.
>
> Now that the enemy has shown that they.
> And in sailing so close.
> In having simply sailed.
>
> [...]
>
> Because if the enemy did.
> If the enemy chose.
> If, at some point, at length, the enemy.

Curtailed sentences such as these also recall a sense of the verbatim, of overheard phrases and snatches of conversation. These accumulate to create a larger, background ambience: where what we read is possibly reporting the speaker's father himself, perhaps recreating his auditory environment or even a combination of both. While Hinsey's treatise reaches towards an articulation of the macropolitical, Morgan seeks to diffuse the ideological power of his subject matter (the nuclear warhead) through a diminuition of scale. So a cache of bombs is compared to "matchsticks / lying snug in their box / their smooth pink heads" yearning to be set "ablaze".

This strategy is repeated, effectively, elsewhere, in parenthesised sections that counterpoint and compare military technology, variously with the agrarian via "the narrowmindedness of combine harvesters", the human as "long-distance runner", the animal, as a "column of unblinking vultures", or the domestic, with missiles that "nestle together / stacking like paper cups".

In this manner the description of "An air-show, sunkissed and sticky, its hot concrete / bordered with gaudy spectators" zooms in on a missile, a "curious giant that looks like a fighter". There is a strange, almost eerie compassion that emerges, when we consider a nuclear weapon to be:

> Like a pony made to turn tight circles
> not by gentle persuasion but by
>
> the sharpness of the bit that tugs
> and cuts into the corners of its mouth.

Rather than compartmentalising the sections, Morgan allows the text to flow, just as the missiles, which paradoxically (and thankfully) never do quite flow. There is a fluidity and musicality inherent even in the title *Assurances*, where military duty transforms to a softer understanding of civilian care. While the approach could not be more different, there is an elegiac mood in both collections: in Hinsey it becomes explicit as an 'Elegy for Thought', while *Assurances* mourns the loss of the human, which even in the most compromised scenario, is "preferable to automation, to the effortless flick of a switch".

> *Karen McCarthy Woolf's latest collection is* Seasonal Disturbances *(Carcanet, 2017).*

REPOSSESSION

Beverley Bie Brahic, The Hotel Eden, *Carcanet, £9.99,*
ISBN 9781784106102
Kit Fan, As Slow As Possible, *Arc, £8.99,* *ISBN 9781911469438*
Amy Key, Isn't Forever, *Bloodaxe, £9.95,* *ISBN 9781780371719*

Claire Crowther on stand-offs, winged heels and sassy negativity

. . .

The Hotel Eden is Beverley Bie Brahic's fourth book of poetry (she has also published sixteen books of prose and poetry translations) and a cool collection of fragmentary mini-dramas. The title poem, acknowledging Joseph Cornell, a pioneer of assembly art, explains the value of scraps: "From laughter to slaughter the house of objects is repossessed." Scraps may seem dull, "Butt-end of an egg. / The spring from a gutted clock", but the poet can name them otherwise:

> On the tip of God's tongue, the bird waits to be named.
> Profoundly silent, the taxidermist's shop. 'If only,'
> thinks the bird.
> If only what?
>
> *Against* survival. *Against* feathers. *Against* corks-in-bottles. *Against*
> the pathos of stuffed birds. *Against* against.
> ('The Hotel Eden')

That tough attitude transforms many of these small scenes into stand-offs. Brahic shows you some lovely thing: the reflection of the moon, six jars of honey, but then blows gnats of irritation against her lush visuals, as in 'Land's End':

> We sniff the grass that smells
> Fresh cut, watch the brides'
> Stiletto heels stab porous turf.
> The spires of the Golden Gate
> Rise through a frieze
> Of cypress trees

These verbs, "cut", "stab", nip at the idyll as do judgments littering the poem, anti-cultural ("too high heels"), anti-classical ("*Vita brevis* days are long"), until the last line, which presents as romantic but seems to crawl with irritation: "The light is consecrating everything." The poet often lashes a whip. 'The Lady and the Hollyhock' describes bucolic pleasure, "a pretty vision", which develops a sour taste. The last lines spit bathos at the reader: "Underneath a gargoyle / Who's just a water spout."

The first poem, 'Madame Martin and I', depicts an old couple spraying roses and pegging out sheets till the poet/storyteller viciously dispatches one of them in the final stanza:

> He was sick all of a sudden
> He was dead
> And now he's gone
> She says she thinks she hardly knew him.

Reversing that nice to nasty shock, in the final poem, 'The Back Road', the narrator takes a different route home via the panoramic view, but finds only shade and mud there, so gets back on her usual track, where at last she sees unappreciated beauty:

> Beside a slope of gently blazing vineyards
> Where *grappillons* still hang –
>
> Grapes for the gleaners.

Lesson in Wordsworthian Romanticism? Perhaps. But how menacing do you find the verb "hang"? Is "blazing" ever a gentle adjective? Grappillons are late grapes, more acid than earlier bunches but worth picking. Sometimes Brahic's professional vexation bubbles up in rage as in 'States of Siege', a powerful political poem:

> What poetry matches a litany of facts?
>
> *another three soldiers and an Afghan*
> *interpreter killed in two blasts* – Globe & Mail

What she asks of the world and clearly rarely gets, Brahic demands of herself. 'States of Siege' ends with this: "Just give us the facts / In their armoured personnel carriers".

As Slow As Possible, Kit Fan's second collection and a Poetry Book Society Recommendation, flies through eras and cultures. A biographical note reads: "his poetry moves between Hong Kong and European cultural histories, he moves amphibiously between poetry and narrative fiction." Here, as an example, is a chair speaking in 'A Chair from Buddha Mountain':

> I was born in the seventh year of the second millennium
> up the Pearl River Delta in the city of Foshan – Buddha
>
> Mountain – where two-thirds of the world's chairs are born
> every year in my hometown.

The gift of inheritance in 'Anatomical and Human Sciences' runs through Genesis, Galen, Mascagni and *Gray's Anatomy* to our time in the poet's childhood experience of medical examination. Fan summarises this flow:

> [...] from the seed of the first apple springs the tree
> of the cross rustling in the wind where a generation of green mouths
> passes secret messages to one another
> like Chinese whispers.

Fan has winged heels but he is not frenzied:

We saunter
through the road of open tombs, unnamed
by their weathered stones. Here a trace of Adam hiding
in the leaves and there a firstborn dangling
from a sword. Christ was here once, attending a funeral.
('Les Alyscamps')

There is an ongoing admission of rupture, endorsed by the geography of Fan's life experience; ironically, it knits the collection together. A majority of the poems contain words such as "not", "no", "without", "nothing". Scene-setting using negatives is common: "There was a time when we were not here / Not stirring the primal scene, not stealing the thunder / from some god" ('Brueghel's Trees'). Anaphora hammers the negatives:

What do the shadows remember?
Not the fireworks.
Not the laser beams.
Not the moth in fire chasing its own shadow.
('To the Shadow-Millions')

With its lost civilisations, its many negatives, and even clichés such as "no substitute" ('Don Kowloon'), "nothing at all" ('The Burning of Books'), this book is a dream of negative thought, a book of not. Here are the last lines of the last poem, 'White on White':

[...] this fog
on cloud on snow is no less
than a blind spot in an absent
mind
crossing
out a figure
on an empty field no more
than one decimal place away, a
substance of a thing that has no
shadow but a yearlong full stop
rounding on and off December.

It's brave to finish a collection with nothing more to say.

There are many ways to be negative in poetry and Amy Key's way, in her second collection *Isn't Forever*, is sassy. From the title on, her demeanour says take me or leave me, you'll have to leave me anyway, and I'm dealing with it. 'I do not need the sea to love me back' is an example:

> I went to the sea
> It was a nearby calamity I had a way with
> I felt it on me like the breath of a cold baby
> It shimmied like voile over a warm radiator
>
> I lay down on the pebbles
> I wanted to have the muscle of a limpet
> To adhere
> And never be washed away

The poem ends "I waited for the sea to notice me / ~~But the sea never notices anyone~~". This is a poem made out of statements, many of them one-liners. It reads simply but the collection makes many more complex attempts to get the poet noticed. 'Announcement and next steps' tries a Latinate way to do the hopeless/hopeful dance:

> In the absence of anything as definitive
> as blood type or maths, I am delighted to declare
> I found the back to the earring, also the mildew is banished,
> albeit temporarily. I want to share this news with you,
> a check against the inventory of living. Personalised
> necklaces point to living. Customisable anything suggests it's all
> worth it.

One of Key's techniques is to mix confessed ignorance with such aphorisms as "The boundaries between self-sabotage / and self-nourish have never been murkier" ('She lacks confidence, she craves admiration insatiably. She lives on the reflections of herself in the eyes of others. She does not dare to be herself.') or "The heart is permanently gory" (The Best Is Yet to Come'). Some you have heard before, some are quotes from other writers; 'Only instead of a star' is a cento with the very awful line, "everything seems very awful". Keys' great-great-aunt Mabel wrote that in her diary and I love her for it.

The structure of the poems, their forms, are so varied that each page hits you almost before you read the poem: gappy, slashed, sectioned, a long drop of short lines, prose. Key's downtrodden unsure personas hold tight to a strong technical hand-up from the mother poet, their emotional frustration rescued by formal dexterity. It is safe to regress among such grand and measured lines as these from 'The Best Is Yet to Come':

I have forgiven the lies I've been told that were intended to soothe me.

~

My enterprise has been: an attempt
to force emotion from things.

~

Feelings often lack structural integrity –

we're all falling into each other.

~

My feelings can't afford the plans I'm making.

~

Another hour wasted in compassion
for the screws in the bedframe.

Isn't Forever is a PBS Wild Card Choice. Sad and sunny, tightlaced and funny, you have to like Amy Key's poems.

Claire Crowther is co-editor of Long Poem Magazine.

THAT UNQUESTIONABLE BLOOM

Tishani Doshi, Girls Are Coming Out of the Woods, *Bloodaxe, £9.95,* *ISBN 9781780371979*
Andrew McMillan, playtime, *Cape, £10,* *ISBN 9781911214373*

Jane Yeh considers gender, desire and violence in two new collections

...

Like a pair of *Masterchef* finalists, Tishani Doshi and Andrew McMillan both have a track record for producing well-regarded work, but each in a very different style: one contemporary and eclectic, the other more classical and restrained. Their latest offerings share the quality of being continuations of their previous themes and approaches. In her wide-ranging third collection, Doshi writes about death and ghosts, beaches and monsoons, Carl Jung and Elizabeth Bishop with wry humour, nimbly juggling the serious and the quotidian. Poem titles such as 'Considering Motherhood While Falling Off a Ladder in Rome' and 'My Grandmother Never Ate a Potato in Her Life' signal the author's unpretentious tone, while her diction is equally lively and flexible: "listen to the slippery / bastard of your own arrhythmic heart", she advises in 'How to be Happy in 101 Days'.

Appealingly smart and self-aware, the poems are dotted with deft one-liners and piquant images. In the coming-of-age tale 'Ode to Patrick Swayze', the speaker recalls, "I wanted to sue my breasts / for not living up to potential"; elsewhere, a group of gossiping women provokes the realisation that

> [...] world over there is a posture
> that involves gleam, that involves lean all the way
> in for a proper bitching.
> ('The Women of the Shin Yang Park Sauna, Gwangju')

The collection itself roams the world over, with poems set in Tamil Nadu, Calcutta [sic], Greece, Sweden, Mexico, and more. Although most of the poems are in free verse, Doshi also plays with sestinas, Golden Shovels (a form using borrowed end-words, invented by Terrance Hayes), and a canzone, as well as frequently resorting to apostrophic address ('To My First White Hairs', 'O Great Beauties!', et al).

While the overall effect is of agreeable variety, it's disappointing to discover that a number of the poems fail to deliver on the promise of their inventive titles, or start well but don't stick their landings. Lines such as "Marvel at how a simple thing can / connect the variegated skeins of time" ('How to be Happy in 101 Days') or "the particularity of yearning / is such that desires are inverted / as soon as they appear" ('To My First White Hairs') strike awkwardly laboured notes; poems like 'Contract' (an epistle to the reader) and 'Find the Poets' (about the value of poetry) just come across as grandiose. By contrast, the best poems here maintain a sharp focus, using imaginative scenarios to generate emotional heft. 'Everyone Loves a Dead Girl' movingly envisions the dead victims of violent men holding parties where they can discuss how they were killed: "and even though they have no names and some of them / have satin strips instead of faces, they all have stories". Doshi balances elegy with bitter wit, her outrage the more fierce for being suppressed. The murdered girls "feel an exhibition of *Wounds You Never / Thought Imaginable* might help contextualise things". The second half of the poem turns its lens on the living, the lucky ones whose daughters are still alive. While satirising their complacency, Doshi also enables us to understand, to empathise:

> [...] how could you not
> hold on to your wrists and listen to *that that that*
> unquestionable bloom? How could you not fall apart
> with relief?

There is a compelling artistry in the way the poet conveys heartbreaking fear and righteous fury in this remarkable piece.

The book's title poem, 'Girls Are Coming Out of the Woods', is likewise a powerful evocation of collective unrest in which the dead rise again, wave after wave of the abused, the molested, the silenced. The poem is a litany of suffering – "girls / found naked in ditches and wells", "forgotten in neglected attics" – that serves a larger purpose; in calling attention to such horrors, Doshi pays tribute to their victims, ensuring that they are "forgotten" no longer. Yet the poem is not only an act of recovery or remembrance. Crucially, Doshi restores agency to the dead girls as they pour out of the woods; rather than resting in peace, they become an unstoppable mob: "They're coming. They're coming". What they're coming for – justice? vindication? vengeance? – is left unsaid, an ambiguity that haunts this tour de force of a poem.

Also partly concerned with male violence, but from another angle, is Andrew McMillan's second book, *playtime*. Written in a fluent, direct style, playtime is an engaging collection of apparently confessional poems that address subjects such as masturbation, anorexia, HIV testing, and hair transplants. McMillan specialises in brief narratives of intimacy and awakening, vivid recreations of experience (real or imagined) that lead to affecting epiphanies. Teenage and prepubescent memories dominate the first half of the collection, with briskly dramatised scenes often set in arenas of budding masculinity, like the changing room or football pitch. McMillan pictures adolescence as lived in a gay, male body as alternately fraught and exciting – "all potential" on the one hand, but also a place of "fear and lust and shame" ('glimpse').

In 'first time sexting', one of a series of poems about sexual initiations ('first time penetration', 'first time with friends', and so on), the virginal speaker finds a like-minded stranger via the internet to exchange fantasies with. Both boys are

> old enough to know what we wanted
> wasn't 'ordinary'   that no one
> taught it us in schools

Same-sex desire, even in the modern world of mobile phones and chat rooms, is still taboo, too out of the ordinary for teenagers to be able or allowed to express it openly. McMillan skilfully uses line breaks here, as throughout, to point up deeper meanings; whereas "old enough to know what we wanted" suggests the boys' hunger for experience, the next line adds in an uncomfortable awareness of their own difference and isolation. At the same time, the very secrecy of their connection is alluring, until the day the speaker accidentally leaves his phone in the classroom at lunch for all to read. Mocked by his fellow students, he runs outside to cry – but then:

> [...] my phone sat vibrating
> in my pocket   like a heartbeat
> refusing to be silent   maybe
> halfwanting to be discovered

The boy's conflicted emotions are encapsulated by this elegant image, in which it turns out that neither his sexual urges, nor his orientation, can be silenced. To be "discovered", while terrifying, also perhaps offers the opportunity to be free.

Underlining McMillan's themes, the words "know", "learn", and "the body", or variations thereof, occur frequently in these poems and form a link to the second half of the collection, which moves into a consideration of adult relationships. McMillan portrays the physicality of sex and the comforts of monogamy, as well as their downsides, through episodic snapshots. In 'inheritance', the speaker describes licking his partner's back, "random lappings   like spots of rain before a storm". As he explains, it's a move he was taught by a previous lover:

> [...] and so it is
>
> I pass it on   and isn't this what humankind
> was made for?

The sense of generosity as embodied through loving touch, of passing on to another the knowledge of pleasure (which is genderless), is rendered in the poem with eloquent simplicity.

In terms of voice and style, *playtime* is very much a follow-up to McMillan's first collection, *physical*, with a similar emphasis on autobiographical frankness and immediacy. It feels churlish to complain when faced with a glut of conventionally well-made poems, but I would have welcomed more variation of approach, more surprise; there's nothing here as risk-taking as the extended sequence called 'protest of the physical', which appeared in his first collection. In fact, the most memorable pieces in *playtime* are the most elliptical ones, depicting charged yet not quite sexual incidents. In 'phonebox', two men waiting for a bus in a downpour squeeze into the only available shelter, sharing a peculiarly forced intimacy; while in 'dancer', the speaker observes the actions of a male dancer with close attention. His "battered / feet leaving their notations on the false wood floor" are as intriguing as his sculpted body, "each movement the beginning of a potential / work of art". The implied "potential" of adultery is never realised in the poem, but rather outweighed by curiosity about the dancer's way of inhabiting the world – a resolution that feels as unexpected as it does right.

Jane Yeh's third collection, Discipline, *will be published by Carcanet in 2019.*

RESPONSE

"We should be resisting at all points the professionalism of anything as gloriously unauditable as writing"

> And why should you want to "stand out"? What's so important about one's writing? [...] I've never found (except in the depressing 'literary scene' sense) poetry to be a competition. Don't you, if you find someone's work interesting, recommend it to your friends? Organic (or perhaps now viral) growth. There's no tape you break after which you can relax [...] I always remember something Val [Raworth] said: "It seems to me fame is just a load of arseholes thinking you're all right."
>
> – Tom Raworth, interviewed in *Misosensitive* (2011)

J.T. Welsch's article, 'The Promise of Professionalism' (*Audit*, 108:3), has the tone of an employee trying to convince themselves that the latest innovation from head office has their best interests at heart. The assertion that we have arrived at a new time for poetry, thanks to a new "creative entrepreneurial" spirit, rings false. It glosses over the notion that the production of art and professionalism have been inherently linked through the ages, the subject of more in-depth analysis by Adorno in the essay 'Culture and Administration' (1978):

> The rigid opposition of culture and administration in thought, the product of a social and spiritual situation which attempts at the same time to force the two together, has nonetheless always been a questionable matter. In art history, it is well known that wherever the artifacts of the past manifest the demand for collective labour – and this extends deep into the individual production of significant architects, sculptors and painters – administration spoke with a decisive voice. For that reason even in the past administration by no

> means lived in a happy harmony with those who today unhesitatingly call themselves the creators of culture – a romantic desire fondly projected backward into history.

Characteristically, Adorno keeps the problem a live one, neither comfortable with the two in opposition nor fetishising art as a sacred or reified object. Welsch quotes Alison Gerber – "artistic practice has undergone an occupational turn" – suggesting that artists now see their work as serious, or as a job. When has it not been serious for those compelled (through whatever motivations) to write? Were Dickinson, Genet, Lispector or Rimbaud less serious about their writing as an occupation than the young artist Gerber invokes?

Welsch's essay makes little reference to how the broader world of work is shifting, in particular its emulation of the cultural industries. Cultural labour has some troubling and familiar features, as Rosalind Gill and Andy Pratt's article 'Precarity and Cultural Work in the Social Factory? Immaterial Labour, Precariousness and Cultural Work' (2013) attests:

> Studies have highlighted a number of relatively stable features of this kind of work: a preponderance of temporary, intermittent and precarious jobs; long hours and bulimic patterns of working; the collapse or erasure of the boundaries between work and play; poor pay; high levels of mobility; passionate attachment to the work and to the identity of creative labourer (e.g. web designer, artist, fashion designer); an attitudinal mindset that is a blend of bohemianism and entrepreneurialism; informal work environments and distinctive forms of sociality; and profound experiences of insecurity and anxiety about finding work, earning enough money and 'keeping up' in rapidly changing fields.

How much of this is applicable to your own situation? The careers of colleagues and friends? With the exception of passionate attachment to the work (one assumes) much of the above could describe any person engaged across the strata of the gig economy, whether a sessional lecturer or an Uber driver. As Richard Florida comments in his book *The Rise of the Creative Class: And How It's Transforming Work, Leisure, Community and Everyday Life* (2002): "As paradigms of entrepreneurial selfhood, 'creatives', as they are now labelled, are the apple of the policymaker's eye, and are recipients of the kind of lip service usually bestowed by national managers on high-tech engineers as generators of value."

Not only are these syndromes of creative labour, they also become the model for late capitalism, as more companies seek to tap into the kind of socialised selfhood that engages workers in their own exploitation. Welsch juxtaposes a traditional view of professionalism, "a top-down process or policing of behaviours", with "savvy individuals" and the possibilities of the "creative ecology". In doing so, he leans heavily into those "paradigms of entrepreneurial selfhood" that find themselves locked in a form of self-policing, through a combination of material deprivation (at no point does Welsch or anyone he cites suggest you can make a reasonable living off poetry) and anxiety about reputational standing. How compelled are you to write and act freely when your income depends on grasping the next tenuous opportunity?

In making his case, Welsch employs the same language that proved so terminal for that great American salesman Willy Loman, without considering the inherent competitiveness it engenders, the cost demanded from that form of professionalism, and most crucially the great appeal art has in eluding what is easily measured and contained. If you want poetry to be, in the words of Jo Bell and Jane Commane's *How to Be a Poet: A Twenty-First Century Guide to Writing Well* (2017), "more fulfilling, life-enriching and creatively satisfying", my advice is you find something else to do. As Blanchot asserted of Kafka's work (in *The Space of Literature*, 1982), "Art is primarily the consciousness of unhappiness, not its compensation."

Welsch suggests that the language of the professional could be weaponised to promote a greater diversity in the poetry community. Initiatives such as the excellent Ledbury Emerging Critics Programme should be applauded for the efforts made to disrupt the established order. However, I would contend that one does not solve inequality by aggressively pursuing a form of self-exploitation, or embracing the language that enables it. We should be resisting at all points the professionalism of anything as gloriously unauditable as writing, embracing instead all its radical possibilities. Leave fame for the arseholes. The best way to be a writer in real life is to be in real life.

Andrew Spragg

CONTRIBUTORS

Fleur Adcock's most recent collection is *Hoard* (Bloodaxe, 2017) • **Simon Armitage**'s latest collection is *The Unaccompanied* (Faber, 2017) • **Baek Eun-seon** is the author of *Possible Worlds* (Moonji, 2016) • **Alison Brackenbury** has published ten books of poetry • **Amy Crutchfield** is an Australian poet living in Melbourne. She is writing her first collection • **Duo Yu** co-founded the prominent 'Lower Body' Movement based in Beijing during the early 2000s • **Kinga Fabó** is a poet, linguist and philosopher based in Budapest. Her books include five collections of poetry in Hungarian • **Andrew Fentham** is a writer and translator based in Cornwall • **Dai George**'s first collection was *The Claims Office* (Seren, 2013). He works as an editor at *Poetry London* and a visiting poet in schools • **Will Harris** is a London-based poet, editor and critic • **Jodie Hollander**'s debut collection is *My Dark Horses* (Liverpool University Press, 2017) • **Fawzia Muradali Kane** is the author of *Tantie Diablesse* (Waterloo, 2011) and *Houses of the Dead* (Thamesis, 2014) • **Vandana Khanna**'s latest publication is *The Goddess Monologues* (Diode, 2016) • **Jae Kim**'s stories have appeared or will appear in *NOON*, *The Collagist* and elsewhere • **Fred Melnyczuk** is a writer based between the Hebrides and London • **Rainie Oet** is is a nonbinary writer. Their work appears in *The Yale Review*, *Shenandoah*, *The Adroit Journal* and elsewhere • **Frank Ormsby**'s latest collection is *The Darkness of Snow* (Bloodaxe, 2017). His next, *The Rain Barrel*, will appear in 2019 • **Pascale Petit**'s seventh collection, *Mama Amazonica* (Bloodaxe, 2017), won the RSL Ondaatje Prize • **Luís Quintais** is a Portuguese-language poet of Angolan origin • **Chris Rice**'s first collection, *Call of Nature*, was published in 2013 • **Sam Riviere** is the author of *81 Austerities* (Faber, 2012), *Kim Kardashian's Marriage* (Faber, 2015) and *Safe Mode* (Test Centre, 2017) • **Lesley Saunders**' translations of Portuguese poet Maria Teresa Horta are forthcoming from Two Rivers Press • **Andrew Spragg**'s recent publications include *Now Too How Soon* (Contraband, 2017) and, with Beth Hopkins, *Dogtown* (Litmus, 2018) • **Fiona Sze-Lorrain**'s latest collection, *The Ruined Elegance* (Princeton, 2016), was a finalist for the *Los Angeles Times* Book Prize • **Ralf Webb** lives and works in London. Recent poems have appeared in the *London Review of Books*, *Test Centre*, *Hotel* and *PAIN* • **Ruth Wiggins**' pamphlet *Myrtle* is published by the Emma Press.

Permissions: Thanks are due to Luís Quintais and Casa Fernando Pessoa in Lisbon for permission to publish Lesley Saunders' translations.

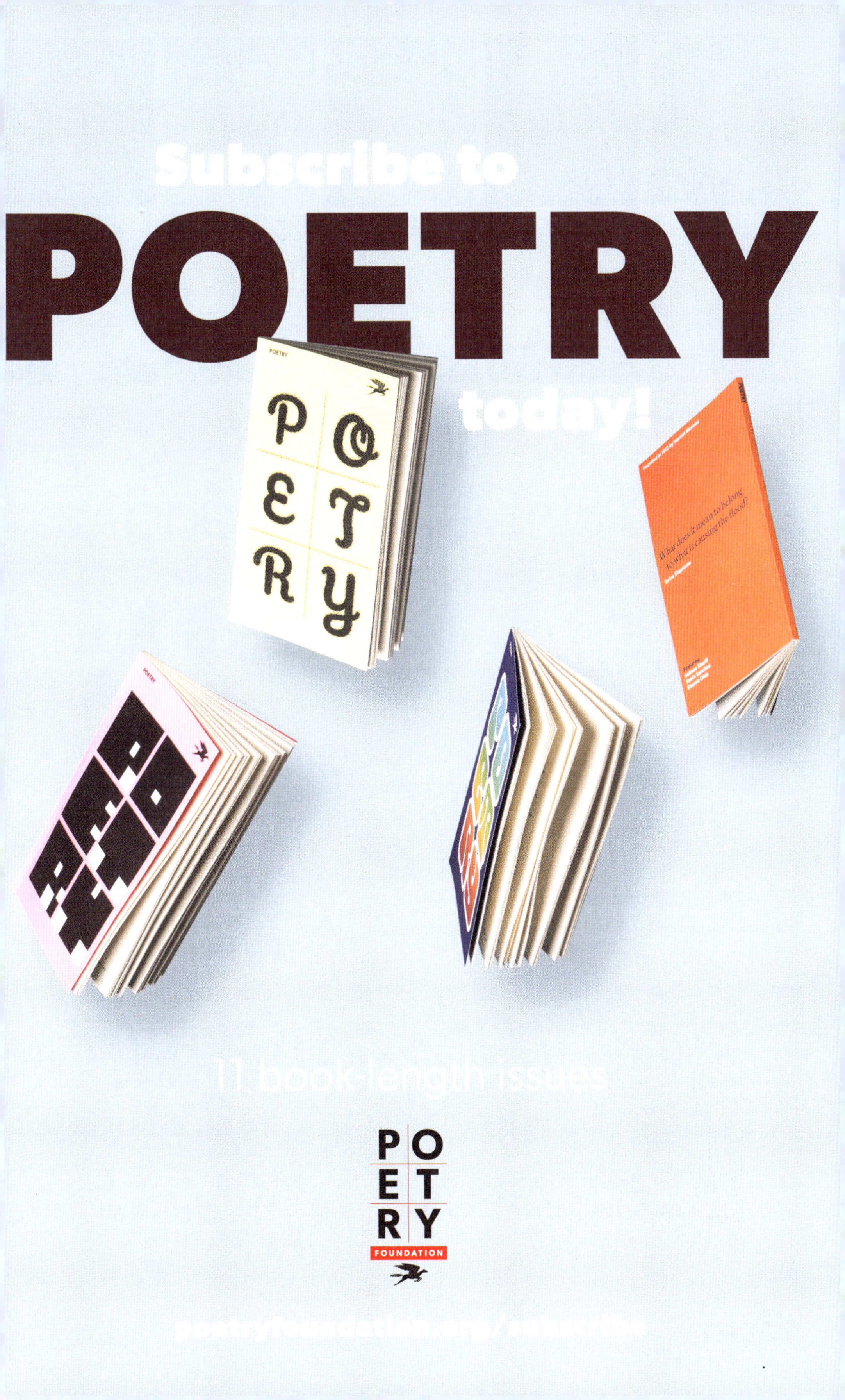
Subscribe to
POETRY
today!
11 book-length issues
POETRY
FOUNDATION
poetryfoundation.org/subscribe

National Poetry Competition

40th Anniversary Readings

Wednesday 20 March 2019 • 7:30pm

Join us for readings and new commissions from some of the UK's finest writers.

The Poetry Society presents a dazzling line-up of ten poets who have gained recognition through the National Poetry Competition's 40-year history.

Book now to hear **Liz Berry**, **Mary Jean Chan**, **Geraldine Clarkson**, **Ian Duhig**, **Fran Lock**, **Sinéad Morrissey**, **Mark Pajak**, **Caleb Parkin**, **Stephen Sexton** and **Jo Shapcott**.

40

NATIONAL
POETRY
COMPETITION

Venue: Kings Place
90 York Way,
London N1 9AG

Tickets: £12.50 / £9.50

Supported by Cockayne Grants for the Arts and The London Community Foundation.

Top, l to r: Sinéad Morrissey; Ian Duhig; Geraldine Clarkson; Caleb Parkin; Jo Shapcott. Below, l to r: Stephen Sexton (photo: Michael Weir); Mary Jean Chan; Fran Lock; Liz Berry; Mark Pajak. *Photos of Geraldine Clarkson and Jo Shapcott by Hayley Madden for The Poetry Society.*

For more information and to book, visit bit.ly/npc40kingsplace

THE POETRY SOCIETY

COCKAYNE

The London Community Foundation

ARTS COUNCIL ENGLAND

Supported using public funding by ARTS COUNCIL ENGLAND